'Send Back the Money!'

The Free Church of Scotland and American Slavery

'Am I not a Woman and a Sister?' American Abolition Token

'Send Back the Money!'

The Free Church of Scotland and American Slavery

Iain Whyte

James Clarke & Co

For Isabel, my wife and life partner,
whose love and support means more than I can ever say.

James Clarke & Co
P.O. Box 60
Cambridge
CB1 2NT

www.jamesclarke.co
publishing@jamesclarke.co

ISBN 978 0 227 17389 3

British Library Cataloguing in Publication Data
A catalogue record is available from the British Library

First published in 2012

Contents

Illustrations

Acknowledgements

I first heard about this 'hidden' episode in mid nineteenth-century Scottish church history from the late Dr Andrew Ross of the University of Edinburgh, whose interest in and knowledge of slavery and abolition greatly assisted me. Andrew directed me to scholarly work on the Free Church of Scotland and slavery by Emeritus Professor George 'Sam' Shepperson in a series of articles in the 1950s. This book owes much to that work and to the personal encouragement and friendship of Professor Shepperson. I am grateful to Mr Owen Dudley Edwards and Professor Stewart J. Brown from the University of Edinburgh, Professor John McIntosh of the Free Church of Scotland College, Emeritus Professor Erskine Clarke, Columbia Seminary, Georgia and Mr Don Martin, editor of *Scottish Local History*, for reading and helpfully commenting on draft chapters. In addition I would like to thank Dr. Eric Graham for his assistance with photographs and in other ways.

In researching the material, I am grateful for the assistance of the staff of the National Library of Scotland, the National Archives, the University of Edinburgh Special Collections, New College Library, Edinburgh, the Edinburgh City Library, the Free Church College Library and the Mitchell Library, Glasgow.

The Strathmartine Trust, St Andrews, provided a generous grant towards research in the Southern States and the Drummond Trust 3, Pitt Terrace, Stirling, a grant subsidising copies of the book. The Librarian at Columbia Seminary, Georgia and the Charleston City Archivist, Mr Harlan Green, greatly assisted me with material and expertise. Gladstone's Library at Hawarden was a familiar and peaceful haven in which to spend some days of writing. Mr John Scoales, College Officer and Property Manager at the Free Church has given generously of his time and expertise and I wish to extend a particular word of thanks to him. Finally, it has been a pleasure to work with Adrian Brink and Bethany Churchard at James Clarke (Lutterworth Press) in the preparation of both text and illustrations.

The First General Assembly of the Free Church of Scotland: Signing the Act of Separation
and Deed of Demission at Tanfield May 1843 by David Octavius Hill
The original painting is in the Free Church College, Edinburgh

Introduction
A Church with Freedom but no Money

At two-thirty in the afternoon of 18 May 1843 the General Assembly of the Church of Scotland was about to begin. Dr David Welsh, that year's Moderator,[1] took his place in the chair in St. Andrews Church, George Street, in the centre of Edinburgh. Welsh was followed by the arrival of the High Commissioner, the representative of the Queen, attended by a military escort. The National Anthem was played. There was an electric air of anticipation in the packed galleries as Welsh, a distinguished Professor of Church History in the University of Edinburgh, rose to his feet. According to the usual form of procedure followed by Scotland's national church at its annual 'parliament' he began:

> This is the time for making up the role, but in consequence of certain proceedings affecting our rights and privileges – proceedings which have been sanctioned by Her Majesty's Government and by the Legislature of the country; and more especially in respect that there has been an infringement on the liberties of our Constitution, so that we could not constitute this Court without a violation of the terms of Union between Church and State in this land, as now authoritatively declared – I must protest against our proceeding further.[2]

Welsh then read from a document that invited Commissioners (delegates) chosen to 'represent the Church of Scotland to leave the room and separate from the Establishment', which, it claimed, had interfered 'with conscience', dishonoured 'Christ's crown' and rejected 'His sole and supreme authority as King in His Church'. He then laid the protest on the table, bowed to the Queen's Commissioner, and left the Church, accompanied by Dr Thomas Chalmers, probably the best known minister in the Kirk, and other Commissioners.

According to eye witnesses, there was a loud cheer from the galleries. As ministers and elders left their seats and went out into George Street a cry went up 'They come! They come!' The expected split in the Church had finally taken place and the stream of men wound its way to a hall at Tanfield over a mile away where they were eagerly greeted by another crowd of spectators. Immediately Chalmers was elected as the first Moderator of the Free Church of Scotland. *The Deed of Demission,* the final break with the Church of Scotland, was signed on 23 May, an historic act commemorated in a famous painting by Octavius Hill. No less than 480 ministers had given up their livelihoods and made themselves and their families homeless for the sake of their conscience. What had led to such a drastic step?

Kirk and State in conflict

The Church of Scotland has a history and constitution as a national church that is totally different to its counterpart in England. The struggle to maintain spiritual independence was characterised by those such as Andrew Melville who told King James VI (James I of England) in 1596 that there were 'two kings and two kingdoms' in Scotland and that 'Christ Jesus' was 'the head of the church whose subject King James VI is'. When the Stuart monarchy tried to impose Episcopal authority on the land, it required draconian military rule to control those who swore a Covenant to resist. The victory of the Dutch King William over the Roman Catholic King James VII at the Battle of the Boyne in 1690, albeit with papal troops and money, led to a settlement giving a permanent guarantee for Presbyterian church order in William's northern kingdom, one preserved amidst whatever other freedoms were lost in the Act of Union between Scotland and England in 1707.

For some years this arrangement worked well. In the meantime two different parties had taken root within the Church of Scotland. The Moderate, or Establishment, group took a conservative approach that upheld the traditions of the Kirk, maintaining in each parish 'the ordinances of religion', the sacraments of Baptism and Holy Communion, proper moral discipline over all within the parish bounds and preaching with scholarly exposition of the scriptures. The Evangelical party sought to evangelise the 'unchurched', welcomed enthusiastic fervour in gospel meetings and even in church, promoted Sunday Schools and other vehicles of Christian Education, and sought missionary opportunities abroad. Most of this was met with disapproval by many Moderates and the unofficial division was evident in the General Assembly of the Kirk whose debates and votes every year reflected swings in the influence of the different parties over that final court of the Church of Scotland.

Of course divisions in Presbyterianism were not new. From the early seventeenth century splinter groups had formed over doctrine or church practice and by the early nineteenth century a substantial number of congregations in Scotland had seceded from the mother church, mainly in order to disassociate themselves from any dependence on, or answerability to, the state. This situation was partly occasioned by the Patronage Act of 1712, which reasserted the right of the crown or landowner to appoint ministers to parishes, something that had been abolished in the 1690 Settlement.

The king or queen often acted in their capacity as a landowner, all of whom held the 'patronage' of providing for and maintaining the parish churches, their ministers, and manses for the latter to live with their families. It was never easy to hold in tension the responsibility of the rulers for maintaining the Kirk and the spiritual independence so valued by it and so dramatically instanced by Andrew Melville. Some notorious cases of interference by patrons nearly caused a split in the mid eighteenth century. But whilst the Moderates held sway in the Assembly, the annual appeals to the crown to have the Patronage Act repealed, were only formal ones and ceased to be made altogether by the 1780s. The increasing influence of the group in the Church now known as the 'Non-Intrusion Party' led to a measure known as the Veto Act (or Act on Calls) being passed in the General Assembly in 1834, heralding what became known as 'the ten years conflict.'[3]

The Veto Act declared that congregations had to be consulted prior to the induction, or appointment, of a minister in a parish. This was seen by the Church of Scotland as a guarantee of its powers as far as Parliament was concerned. The Edinburgh-born Lord Brougham, former Lord Chancellor of England, stated in the House of Lords his belief that the Act had clarified and protected the important question of Patronage 'on a footing advantageous to the community' and 'safe and beneficial to the Establishment'.[4] Yet these very words masked deep rumblings in the system that were to break out dramatically within some months of Brougham's confident words.

In the autumn of 1834, when a reformed Parliament in Westminster was heralding progress on many fronts, not least with the abolition of slavery in the British Empire, Lord Kinnoul presented a minister to the congregation of Auchterarder in Perthshire, five-sixths of whom protested and asked for an alternative nominee. The Presbytery refused to ordain Kinnoul's choice and after a long vacancy without a minister, the Court of Session upheld the landowner's right to appoint the minister of his choice, a decision supported by the House of Lords in 1839. In the years between 1834 and 1839 there had been 150 vacancies in Church of Scotland parishes. The great majority were filled without incident either because the landowner paid attention to the Veto Act's provisions or because the parishioners had no strong grounds for objection to these ministers. It was, however, shaky ground on which to proceed.

Dr Chalmers, then Professor of Divinity at the University of Edinburgh and the leader of the 'Non-Intrusion' Party in the Church, had been Moderator of the 1832 Church of Scotland General Assembly. He sought to go slowly in asserting the Kirk's spiritual independence, but the House of Lords's decision and the strident way in which the London lawmakers had declared their impatience with the Church radicalised him enough to persuade the Assembly to negotiate with the Government over the separation of civic and spiritual power. In the meantime the Moderate dominated Presbytery of Strathbogie in Aberdeenshire agreed by seven votes to four to obey the Court of Session and ordain the nominee of the patron, despite the General Assembly's direction of 1838 to reject a man who had only received one vote.

The Whig Government was replaced by a Tory one in 1841 led by Sir Robert Peel, a man who once had been on friendly terms with Chalmers but who, with Sir James Graham, Secretary of State for Scotland, was determined to support the status quo and resist any change in the law. The 1842 General Assembly, which continued to be dominated by the 'Non-Intrusion' Party, adopted a deliverance which came to be known as the Claim of Right, quoting the 1690 Settlement and the Westminster Confession of faith drawn up by Presbyterians in the time of Charles I, and asserting the independence of the Church in all matters spiritual. It was sent to James Graham and after his rejection, the matter was referred to Parliament.

Cracks Appear and a Split becomes Inevitable

Meanwhile a Convocation held in November 1842 led by Chalmers brought together a large number of ministers who recognised the need to stand firm on the 'Non-Intrusion' principle and 423 agreed to break with the Church of Scotland if Parliament would not recognise the Claim of Right. Preparations were under way for the organisation and financing of the now almost inevitable Free Church of Scotland. Throughout the winter meetings were held in the towns and deputations sent into rural areas, local committees were set up and funds collected. At least one church was built in Edinburgh to receive the congregation of St. George's which had pledged to follow its minister Dr Robert Candlish, soon to be one of the most prominent leaders in the Free Church.

In March 1843 the House of Commons rejected the Claim of Right by 221 votes to 76, although of the 37 Scottish members of parliament, 25 were in favour and 12 against. There was no more room for negotiation. Two questions remained in the light of the impending General Assembly of the Church of Scotland. If the Presbyteries nomination of Commissioners (delegates) gave the 'Non-Intrusionists' (effectively the Popular Party) a majority, would they simply force a vote to end all connection with the state? And if, as happened for the first time in the ten years of contention, the supporters of 'Non-Intrusion' failed to secure a majority in the Assembly, would those 423 who pledged to leave the church actually do so at the moment of decision?

According to well established custom the retiring Moderator, having served his year of office, takes the chair on the opening day of the General Assembly and then hands over to his successor. The dramatic break in 1843 when Dr Welsh declared that he could not regard this as a Free Assembly and left St. Andrews Church was described by the judge and sympathetic chronicler Henry Cockburn in these proud but sombre terms:

> As soon as Welsh, who wore his Moderators dress, appeared in the street and people saw that principle had really triumphed over interest, he and his followers were received with the loudest acclamations. But amidst this exultation there was much sadness and many a tear, many a grave face and fearful thought, for no-one could doubt that it was with sore hearts that these ministers left the Church, and no thinking man could look on the unexampled scene and behold that the temple was rent without pain and sad forebodings.[5]

Cash and Credibility – The Transatlantic delegation

One of the first considerations for the new Free Church, with its need to provide for over 400 ministers, their housing and that of their families, to buy or lease land and build churches, to say nothing of support for education and outreach work at home and overseas, was the obvious necessity of money. As in many enterprises, Dr Chalmers took the lead by organising funds for ministry, building, education, and missions. In the years 1843/44 the Free Church of Scotland raised £363,871, a staggering total only surpassed twenty-one years later. The drama of 1843 and the wave of public support had obviously led to great and spontaneous generosity but the worry was that once the excitement had died down, would the rate of giving also fall away? [6]

The Free Church leaders were aware that their cause had attracted support not only throughout Scotland, but far beyond. Yet they were equally aware that such support needed to be carefully nurtured in the difficult years ahead. To build on what they had done would need careful advocacy. They could not expect the Church of Scotland to wish them well in their departure from it. Opposition and obstruction would certainly come from those with landed and establishment interests but that would most likely be matched by the more subtle propaganda designed to paint the Free Church in a poor light.

Not only would there be the need to commend their case to the people of Scotland but also to do so elsewhere. One of the very first steps to take the Church's case to a wider audience was made by the decision to send a delegation to the United States within months of the foundation of the Free Church.

Five men were chosen to represent the Free Church in this delegation. Dr Robert Burns was minister of the Laigh Kirk in Paisley, a pulpit occupied in the previous century by Rev. John Witherspoon, who later became President of Princeton and a signatory to the American Declaration of Independence. Burns was a friend of Thomas Chalmers and had been Secretary of the Glasgow Missionary Society. Dr William Cunningham was the best known member of the delegation. Cunningham had been a minister in Greenock and Edinburgh and had recently been appointed as Professor of Church History and Divinity at the new Free Church College. The previous year he had been awarded an honorary doctorate from Princeton. Rev. William Chalmers was minister of Dailly Parish Church in Ayrshire. At the Disruption he had led a number of his parishioners out of the church to worship in the open air and the planned new Free Church in Dailly had not yet been completed. The other two members who were asked to go to America were from Dundee. Mr Henry Ferguson, an elder and prominent merchant in the city, was to accompany Cunningham in the early stages of the tour. Rev. George Lewis, the minister of St. David's Free Church and already a noted writer, who was to undertake the most extensive journey of them all in America, completed the group.

Their remit was to travel widely and commend the Free Church to the American churches, especially those of the Presbyterian persuasion. They were not to seek money specifically but it was certainly assumed that part of the hoped-for support as a result of their labours would include financial contributions. They would have to expect some suspicion and outright opposition, but none of them were prepared for their reception of modest donations to the cause entangling them in an issue which was splitting the American church as it was to split the nation and whose ripples would very evidently be felt before long on Scottish shores.

Chapter 1
A Delegation Warmly Received

To Dr Smyth's activity and hearty zeal in our cause we were deeply
indebted during our stay. Nothing was wanting on his part to
awaken both our fellow countrymen and American Christians to the
principles and issues of the recent struggles in Scotland
Impressions of America and the American Churches
from the Journal of Rev. G. Lewis 1845

Fertile Ground
In the mid nineteenth century the American War of Independence
was still a vivid memory in the lives of tens of thousands across
the Atlantic. Rebellion against a supposedly tyrannical system had
become a sacred duty in the minds of patriotic Americans, who
hugged to their ideological chests the mantra of freedom from
control. However ironic this would be, not least to millions of African
Americans who suffered under the bonds of enslavement, it was so
deeply rooted that any British citizen who sought to free themselves
from restrictions on their liberty, might expect moral support from
those who had any power and influence in the new world of the
United States.

No part of this was more powerfully rooted than freedom of
religion. The epic journey of the Pilgrim Fathers in 1619 would
be followed by many other communities of faith who had found
themselves in a minority in European nations, where they were at
best marginalised by the official religion of the state, or at worst
persecuted with threats to their lives. The irony in this situation was
often lost in the new world. Puritan America would see the most
appalling witch hunts of those who supposedly did not conform to
the narrowest of doctrines or morality. Anti-Catholic prejudice was
such that even in 1960 the election of a Roman Catholic President
seemed as much of a shift in the template as the election of an African
American one in 2008. Nevertheless, the belief in 1844 that America
was a model for religious tolerance and would salute any who made
a brave and sacrificial stand for their faith in the face of the religious
establishment, was overwhelmingly strong.

Such ripe soil was attractive in the seventeenth century for English dissenters as for French Huguenots, Dutch Protestants fleeing the Spanish empire, and Romanian Unitarians later defying the Orthodox Church. No group at this time, however, were more in tune with the Free Church delegation than the numerous and widespread Scottish communities in the United States. Many had been there for generations, maintaining the traditions of the 'old country.' In recent decades, the 'improvements' made to Scottish agriculture by the introduction of sheep farming had led to tens of thousands of Highland and Lowland small-tenant farmers being evicted from their lands and forced to a seek exile in North America. The orders for this eviction had come from landowners, some of whom lived on the same land as their tenants, but many of whom lived far out of sight of the events. Some, like the Duke of Sutherland, whose estate became the scene of some of the most notorious of the evictions, lived much of the time in London. In 1852 the American anti-slavery author Harriet Beecher Stowe, whose *Uncle Tom's Cabin* by this time was a best-seller, visited the Sutherlands at Dunrobin Castle in the northeast and wrote warmly of the Duchess's support for the cause of black liberty – yet another of history's ironies.[1]

Why should those who were exiled by the Clearances, as they became known, be inclined to give support to the Free Church of Scotland? It was not because they were naturally rebellious or militant – in fact many had maintained an almost myopic loyalty to those inheritors of the clan system, until it became all too obvious that there was not a shred of paternalistic care left buried beneath the overriding passion to take full advantage of profit. Peaceful resistance, or that accompanied simply by the threat of wooden sticks, was met by the full rigours of British military might when called into the service of the lairds. Few were as courageous or foolhardy as the tenant of the Duke of Sutherland who responded to the call to arms in the newly formed Argyll and Sutherland Highlanders – 'since your Lordship has preferred sheep to men, let sheep defend you'. In the face of such injustice, the best equipped to defend the rights of the tenant, armed as they would be with the prophetic heritage of Old Testament figures, would be their spiritual leaders. Who better able to quote to the powers that be those words from the prophet Isaiah: 'Woe betide those who add field to field until everyone is displaced and there is none left in the land but yourselves', but the parish ministers of the Church of Scotland?[2]

With few honourable exceptions, there was at best a deafening silence on the part of those whose livelihoods depended on the patronage of the very men who were busy substituting sheep for

Second Presbyterian Church, Charleston, South Carolina

tenants. Not a few found advantageous passages of scripture to quote in support of obedience to lawful authority, even when that authority had totally abandoned the kind of responsibilities for those under him that were implicit in Calvin's *Institutes*, let alone St. Paul's defence of the authority of the Roman Empire. Donald Sage, witness of the Sutherland clearances, said that the Church of

Scotland ministers 'discharged what they called their duty. . . they did not scruple to introduce the name of the Deity; representing him as the author and abettor of all the foul and cruel proceedings carried on'. [3]

One of the reasons that the Free Church of Scotland has a hold in those parts of Scotland most denuded in the Clearances, is that the Church of Scotland has not easily lived down the betrayal of those days. Even if few of those who left on the ships plying across the Atlantic had by 1844 managed to achieve power or influence in the United States, there were many Scots who preceded them and would find good cause to see the Free Church's separation from the Church of Scotland as a stand for justice and freedom against tyranny – the tyranny supported by the old established religion.

Of course the Presbyterianism which the Free Church delegates encountered in the United States had its own fragmentation. The Northern and Southern varieties were only just held together by compromises paralleled in the political system. A united Presbyterian Church in slave-ridden America was to prove in the end as impossible a body to sustain as a slavery-divided United States. Slave-ownership was that question which, however much they attempted to avoid it, would dog the Free Church delegates when they returned home.

Presbyterians in the United States divided in 1837 between groups entitled Old School and New School. The Old School represented traditional Calvinism. This was reinterpreted by the New School, who rejected some of the harsher doctrines, and drew on the Scottish 'common sense' philosophy that advocated moral government. At the 1837 General Assembly in Philadelphia the Old School majority expelled New School members who published a more liberal theological declaration. The Supreme Court of Pennsylvania decided that the Old School were the true representatives of Presbyterianism. New School members tended to challenge slavery and many of their members were active in abolitionist circles.

Princeton and far beyond

William Cunningham and Henry Ferguson were the first to arrive in the United States in December 1843. Cunningham, although only thirty-three, had already made his mark as a church leader. After ministries in Greenock and Edinburgh he had, just months before setting out to America, been appointed to a Chair at the new Free Church College. He had suffered a tragic family bereavement when his four-year-old son Willie died of whooping cough just weeks before he was due to sail. Nonetheless, having made this commitment to the church, he sought to fulfil it and he didn't return home until mid-May 1844. Robert Burns, William Chalmers and George Lewis came over at the beginning of 1844. Most of the delegation returned by the time of the Free Church General Assembly in May, but Lewis stayed until July making by far the most extensive journey of all through two dozen states, North and South, and visiting Toronto and Montreal in Canada.

Although all of the delegation were mandated to present the case for the Free Church and 'gather in the fruits of American liberality', Cunningham's first priority was to visit what the Education Committee described as 'Some of the most eminent of the American Theological Institutions'. His recent appointment to a Chair at New College meant that he was seen as an ideal candidate to assess what could be learnt by the Free Church from those who had been teaching theological students for some decades. Early in the visit to the States no less than four members of the delegation arrived at that crucial centre of Presbyterian theological education, Princeton in New Jersey. Princeton's Scottish connections stemmed from Rev. John Witherspoon from Paisley, its sixth and best known President (Principal) from 1768 to 1797.

Cunningham stayed twice with the current President of the College, Dr Charles Hodge. He found it a rewarding experience. The President, an Old School Theologian, and a notoriously shy man, was later to engage in a vehement attack on Charles Darwin the naturalist. He told a mutual friend that he had rarely met anyone whom he held in such high regard on such a short acquaintance as Cunningham. Later he wrote that having him as a guest was a highlight of his life. A contemporary observer at Princeton described Cunningham 'altogether the most satisfactory foreigner I have seen . . . he has no airs of patronage'.[4] Certainly no Free Church leader could afford to be seen with such a characteristic. A visiting Professor, James Alexander, attended an hour long speech and was mesmerised by:

> Indescribable Scotch intonation (but little idiom) and convulsion of body, but flowing, elegant language, and amazing power in presenting argument. Though his manner is rugged and uncouth and he has no sign of imagination, yet when he gets to the subject of religion he is so scriptural and so sound that one is affected by what he says. I have seldom listened to a man with more instruction.[5]

Ferguson accompanied Cunningham to Princeton. At first Alexander was 'thunderstruck' by the sight of a man who had 'the dress and ways of a weaver' and was puzzled by the fact that he had been specially appointed to accompany Cunningham on the recommendation of Thomas Chalmers, already a revered figure at the college. 'My wonder ceased' he wrote 'when I heard him. He spoke an hour and three quarters by the watch; I wish it had been twice as long'. Despite Ferguson cutting a seemingly comical figure and with poor elocution, Alexander and his brother were deeply moved by his eloquence and passion. Although he wrote 'it is utterly vain for me to give you any idea of the degree of his [Ferguson's] power' and described his diction as 'elegant and sublime', he added, 'and yet he is only a merchant of Dundee'.

Cunningham preached a number of times at Princeton. On 16 March his text from St. Paul's second letter to the Corinthians, chapter five, verse fourteen – 'If one died for all then all died' was described as 'a noble sermon as plain and unillustrated as before but mighty in argument and robustly eloquent'. The impression he gave to his hosts, who judged him to be in his 40s, (he was 38) was of a mature and senior figure in the Free Church, with the necessary gravitas not evident in some others in the delegation. In a letter dated 20 Feb Alexander wrote, 'The Scotch delegates thicken upon us. We have had Rev. Dr Burns and Elder Ferguson and we are daily expecting Lewis, who has arrived at New York'. After Robert Burns preached, the comments were 'his manner in the pulpit (gestures excepted) is more outré than Cunningham's. But his sermon was noble, rich, scriptural and evangelical and in diction elegant . . . his closing prayer was seraphic'. Lewis, who was asked to conduct worship shortly after he arrived at Princeton, was described by Alexander as 'a gentlemanly man' who gave 'a delightful gospel sermon'.

With such goodwill evoked by the four delegates at Princeton, some tangible support was almost bound to result. In fact 500 dollars were subscribed right at the beginning of the visit – a reasonable sum from what was still a modestly endowed institution with a fraction of the students it would have when it achieved full University status.

The four delegates were never again to come together in America. William Chalmers made his focus the mid-West and did not join the others at Princeton but was later to be with Lewis at the crucial Assembly of the Presbyterian Church in the slave-state of Kentucky. Robert Burns spent a good deal of time in Canada. He collected two-thousand pounds for the Free Church in Montreal and when Lewis was departing from Halifax, he learnt from various people how successfully Burns had pled the cause in Nova Scotia. Some of the Canadians wanted him to be the first Free Church minister of the prestigious Knox Presbyterian Church in Toronto, and their Synod invited him to develop a ministry to native Canadians. It would not be long until he accepted a teaching call in Toronto.

Before going north, Burns had secured an interview with the present incumbent at the White House, John Tyler, a former Governor of Virginia and the first Vice President to inherit the Presidency, holding it despite the resignation of his entire cabinet. Tyler, an Episcopalian, appeared to be impressed with the Free Church struggle for independence and commented 'in the United States we allow every man to get to heaven as best he can, if he gets there at all'.[6]

William Cunningham took a heavy programme on himself but mainly stayed in the east, visiting Washington, Philadelphia, Baltimore and Virginia. He was to have preached before members of Congress but illness prevented this. He was accompanied for much of the time in the eastern states by Robert Burns, but the two men did not adopt the same approach. Cunningham's style was that of the elder statesman, concentrating on the case for the Free Church to be recognised as the conscience of Scotland. He was treated almost as a surrogate Thomas Chalmers. In Lafayette College in Pennsylvania the Trustees told him before he left for home on 1 May that they would award a Doctorate to any minister in Scotland praised by him.

By contrast Burns, in a letter immediately after his arrival in Princeton, wrote that his 'testifying processes' began there and was part of his presentation. He admitted that Cunningham saw personal testimony as outside their remit, and had no intention of following him. The later success of Robert Burns in the north and Canada was probably increased by the principles of the Disruption being leavened a little by some personal witness.

The most extensive traveller, and one who left the most complete record of his journeys, was George Lewis. Lewis began by visiting as many churches in New York as possible, and at the end of each service tried to get opportunities to commend the cause of the Free Church. This intensive programme delayed his visit to Princeton, after which he also had an audience with the President. Tyler asked after Dr Chalmers's age and health. 'You are a people that go through with a thing', said the President to Lewis. 'John Knox did it and I fancy you are following his steps'.

While in Washington, Lewis and Burns attended and spoke to

the Baltimore Methodist Episcopal Church conference. For both men this was their first exposure to African American Christians and their short contributions were, in Lewis's account, 'received by many 'Amens' and 'oh, ohs.' When Lewis preached to the Conference on 16 March he was discomfited by what he thought were inappropriate interjections but was moved both by the messages of support from the conference and the generous gifts from what was a very poor church.

After visiting Washington, George Lewis and Henry Ferguson entered the Deep South. There they were to encounter the warm and generous hospitality that awaited any traveller, particularly from the 'old country', who was polite enough not to violate the code by raising questions about the South's 'peculiar institution'. Their host and guide in Charleston, South Carolina, was the Irish-born Dr Thomas Smyth, influencial minister of the Second Presbyterian Church and a friend of Thomas Chalmers. Lewis was later to write:

> to Dr Smyth's activity and hearty zeal in our cause we were
> deeply indebted during our stay. Nothing was wanting on his
> part to awaken both our fellow countrymen and American
> Christians to the principles and issues of the recent struggles
> in Scotland'.

But in some churches the Disruption was a sensitive issue and almost as taboo as the topic of slavery. Lewis declined one invitation to preach in a so-called 'Scotch Church' under these conditions and a Methodist minister who had left Scotland in 1832, argued with Lewis and Ferguson, maintaining that they should have fought patronage from within the Kirk.

Seeing slavery and hearing from the Presbyterians

In early April Lewis set off for Savannah, Georgia and then went through Alabama to New Orleans. Much of his travelling was by boat and he had the most first-hand experience amongst all the delegates of experiencing slavery in the raw rather than at a distance. He saw over one hundred slaves on the journey to Charleston and was struck by one young girl recognising her sister on the boat, from a separate batch of 'merchandise'. On another river trip he engaged some slaves in conversation, sharing a bag of oranges with them and hearing of their fears of being sold in Mississippi. At Montgomery, Alabama, Lewis observed a slave market which even his host showed him 'with shame'. In Savannah, he was told anxiously by a 'coloured' minister to avoid the topic of slavery and a Scottish immigrant who, in Lewis's estimation 'had learnt to accommodate himself to the evils around him' asked Lewis 'are you come to spy on me?'

From the Louisiana coast Lewis journeyed back north to St. Louis and then to Louisville, Kentucky where the General Assembly of the Presbyterian Church met in mid May. He was joined by Chalmers on 24 May and together they addressed the Assembly, Chalmers on the facts of the disruption and Lewis on the principles. George Lewis reported that the two Scots were unimpressed by the informality and lack of order in the proceedings, although a motion to set up a committee to support the Free Church was unanimously passed. But, said Lewis, 'as much as our hearts were gladdened by this kindly welcome, so much more were we cast down by the reception which the Assembly gave to the question of slavery'.

Strangely enough 24 May 1844 was to see motions from synods on the subject of American slavery presented to the General Assemblies of the Presbyterian Church meeting in Kentucky and the Free Church of Scotland meeting in Edinburgh. The Free Church, as we will see, remitted consideration of the issue to a Committee. The Presbyterian Church in America voted to refuse discussion of the matter by 117 votes to 69. Lewis concluded that the great fear was the break up of the union both in church and state. He was twice asked to preach in Louisville and this time it was slavery rather than the Disruption that was the topic off limits.

While at the Assembly, Lewis asked a delegate whether it was true that state governments forbade the teaching of African Americans to read. 'It is too true' was the reply, 'we are not in this matter a free church but we cannot presently help ourselves'. Lewis retorted that this contradicted the scriptural injunction to all Christians to search the scriptures' and that the calling of the church was 'to tell the civil power to go back to its own place'.

The notes made by Lewis would be published the following year under the title *Impressions of America and the American Churches*. In 1846 a selection of his journal was given a separate imprint as *Slavery and Slaveholders in the United States of America*. How far these were revised in the light of events that were to follow is hard to judge, but George Lewis was considerably exercised by what he had seen of the American churches' attitude to slavery. It is certain that he believed slavery in the United States to be 'milder' than that recently abolished in the West Indies, something on which most modern historians agree. He was encouraged by churches such as the Associate Reformed Synod, which had declared slave-holding a sin, and the Methodists who recently called on a slave-holding bishop to resign. But he was disappointed that although in the previous century the Presbyterian General Assembly had agreed slavery to be 'a great moral evil', nothing had been done about it since then. Even at Princeton, although the leaders were living in a 'free' state, they could not bring themselves to call slavery 'sin', with the consequence of seeing their southern colleagues and even the Old Testament patriarchs as sinners.

Lewis declared that to accept the law prohibiting African Americans from reading and writing was a grave failure of the Presbyterian church. Such a law, for him, was 'a plain violation of its freedom as a church'. His awareness that Presbyterians had not lobbied the legislature or attempted to rouse their congregations on the matter led him to say 'with solemn regret that our Presbyterian brethren in the States have come short of their duty'.

To those who would argue that slavery was sanctioned by scripture, Lewis responded that polygamy was also accepted in the Old Testament and never condemned by Jesus, yet the church today would have no difficulty in expelling polygamists. Although for him it was clear that 'the law of God as given from Sinai contained the germ of all our duties', it was also clear that God 'shed light from age to age'. Such a perspective clearly put George Lewis on the liberal side of the Free Church spectrum. His conclusions on what he called 'the foul spot' (slavery) on the nation and the duty of the Christian church to take strong action against its members who practised it, did not sit any too easily with many of his colleagues in the Free Church. Had he been able to attend the 1844 General Assembly in Edinburgh instead of the one in Kentucky and speak from personal experience, the outcome might have been very different. But already a strong wind had blown from the north and the flames were being fanned in Scotland.[7]

The Wages of Iniquity?

On 2 April a letter was sent to all the delegates from the Executive Committee of the American and Foreign Anti-Slavery Society. It was signed by nine members, including the businessmen brothers Arthur and Lewis Tappan, who together had founded the Society in 1840. Anti-Slavery groups tended to imitate the churches in their propensity to fragment. The Tappans, being opposed to female suffrage and the participation of women in any anti-slavery activities, had parted company with William Lloyd Garrison's American Anti-Slavery Society, which they had both founded. Arthur Tappan was a corresponding member of the Glasgow Emancipation Society, whose minutes indicate a great deal of mutual communication across the Atlantic. He would have been well aware of the travels of the Free Church delegation and the support that they had received in the south as well as the north.[8]

The letter began diplomatically, but rather romantically, by recognising Scotland's stand against 'ecclesiastical and civic tyranny'. In assuring the Free Church of its sympathy and support, it immediately linked that struggle with those 'professed brothers and sisters in Christ' in the Southern States whose situation was far worse than 'The Christian peasantry of Sutherland'. That subtle insertion showed that the Society had done their homework and they continued by a reference to dukes who required their tenants to listen to ministers chosen by them and who were supported in this by the Civil Courts. 'There are no Dukes', the letter continued 'in this republic, but there are thousands of tyrants, some of whom are called 'honourable', who will not allow their slaves to read the Bible or attend upon preaching of their choice, and the courts sustain them in their prohibition'.

Having made the direct connection between the causes in Scotland and America, the Society's letter turned to the prospects of gaining support and encouragement from slave-holders in the south, provided 'you seal your lips against any condemnation of slave-holding', Texts such as 'servants, obey your masters', would be acceptable to slave-holders, but not Paul's exhortation 'give unto your servants that which is just and equal'. The authors compared the complaints against Sir Robert Peel, the British Prime Minister, who would not consent 'that your Scotch brethren shall have the preacher of their choice' with the speech of a senator in South Carolina, who threatened to hang any who advocated that thousands of Presbyterian brethren in slavery should be allowed to read the Bible.

What started in measured tones then became more and more strident in considering the Free Church's receipt of any money at all from congregations which included slave-owners. 'You contemplate carrying that impious gold . . . to lay the foundations of Free Churches and raise roofs which are to echo the voices of Wishart, Hamilton, and Henderson'. 'Building a town with blood' was the implication of the receiving money in this way and of course silence on slavery was the price. 'The fiend' is well able, went the argument, to give tens of thousands because the approval of the Free Church is worth far more. Citing a veteran abolitionist and Free Church leader who died in 1831 they continued, 'If he [the slave-owner] can purchase the silence of the successors of John Knox and Andrew Thomson, if he can number them among is allies, he will think his victory complete.[9]

The Society then turned to an appeal for support for the abolitionists. 'You will hear the abolitionists in this country' they said 'denounced by ministers, elders, and private professors of the Presbyterian Church, as well at the North as at the South'. However, they wished to assure the delegates from Scotland that 'our doctrines and measures . . . are identical with those of Wilberforce, Clarkson, Andrew Thomson and the other worthies who amidst threats, calumny, and violence, carried on the anti-slavery cause in our fatherland, under the Divine blessing, to a glorious consummation'.

However fine that rhetoric was, the Free Church delegation knew all too well that it was over-egging the pudding. Clarkson's life may have been threatened when collecting data in Bristol and Wilberforce and Thomson had been the subject of vicious verbal attacks from the West Indians, but it was nothing compared with the American experience of pastors driven from their parishes, death threats and severe beatings suffered by those who dared to raise the abolition cause, and not just in the deep South.

The letter recognised the support for the abolition cause by 'Christian brethren in England, Ireland, and Scotland' and argued not only that the acceptance of southern assistance by the Free Church would weaken the work of abolition in America, but that it would inhibit the Church from sending strong remonstrances to the American Presbyterians on slavery. It flew off into grand polemic with this warning:

Respected Christian brethren: be warned! You are now sojourning in the house of the serpent. We have, it is true, his slime and his folds in the North but his head and fangs are in the South. Are you in no danger from the fascination of his eye? Beloved guests from our mother country, suffer our frank and friendly exposition. Is not the Free Church of Scotland virtually here in you? Can you fall into grievous error without injuring her? Consider, you left the establishment with nothing but your characters. Houses, lands, salaries – all was left behind except Christian character. Never did that jewel of your souls shine so brightly as in the dark hour when you went forth hearing the reproach of Christ. You are at war with oppression and you come to us for the sinews of war. Can you suppose that the wages of iniquity are of any value to *you*?

However fervent this appeal was, the American and Foreign Anti-Slavery Society obviously realised that it came a little too late. Two of the delegation were on the last lap of their journey and Lewis had already left Charleston, the centre of his tour in the South and the place from where most of the Southern offerings had come. The question they posed at the end of the letter was what the reaction at home might be. 'What will the enemies of the Free Church- the State hirelings – say if you carry home the slave-holder's bounty? They would say that the Free Church of Scotland could not 'swallow the bread of their Sovereign' but were prepared to 'beg a pittance from the pulpits of tyrannical oppression in Washington, Charleston and New Orleans'.

As a final plea, the writers expressed the hope that if their urging to refuse money 'acquired by the sale of American Christians and men made heathens by the cruel system of slavery' was ignored, then on the return of the delegation 'your constituents, the Free Church of Scotland, will refuse to receive the polluted silver and gold and return it to those who gave it'. The 'Send Back the Money' campaign that for a short time was to divide churches, families and communities in Scotland and would see some great orators at packed Scottish meetings had just been launched in New York.

The letter to the delegation was made public through the press in the United States. James Alexander writing on 9 April to a friend commented 'you see the Abolitionists are out upon the Scotchmen for fingering the wages of iniquity [receiving donations] for the Free Church from slaveholders. They will learn a lesson as to the animus of the American anti-slavery men'.[10] Prophetic words for the next year or two in Scotland. But in the meantime two members of the delegation, William Cunningham and Henry Ferguson, were preparing to return home to report to the first General Assembly of the Free Church of Scotland. They had no intention of addressing the issue of slavery, still less to recommend the return of any money gathered during their stay.

Chapter 2
The Elephant in the Room

That they take into their serious consideration the propriety of addressing, in a friendly and brotherly spirit, the Presbyterian and other churches in the United States of America, on the continuance of slavery in that country, and the countenance alleged to be given to it by professing Christians and religious communities
Petition of the Synod of Lothian and Tweeddale to the 1844 General Assembly of the Free Church of Scotland, 1844

Tidings from America

There was an air of expectation at the opening of the first General Assembly of the Free Church of Scotland. Twelve months after the momentous days of the Disruption and overlapping with the Church of Scotland's annual gathering, delegates, or commissioners as they were termed, met in Tanfield Hall, Edinburgh, in May 1844.

At seven o'clock on the evening of 20 May the hall was crowded to overflowing. After worship the Assembly agreed before any other business was transacted to hear Dr William Cunningham's report on the delegation to America. The audience was desperately keen to hear that the Free Church struggle had been reported and approved of across the Atlantic. Cunningham spent little time by way of introduction, apart from offering thanks to Divine Providence for preservation and safe return to his family. 'I may say generally', began his report 'and that statement simple as it may be is somewhat comprehensive – that I have been greatly delighted by my visit to the churches'. Perhaps in anticipation of awkward questions, he disclaimed sufficient time or experience spent in America to form any judgement on the 'general state of affairs or on the state of morality in those interesting and important departments of Christian work' in the Churches there. 'No doubt many men have dogmatised on these subjects' he continued, and 'expressed opinions favourable and unfavourable', but as a stranger he did not intend to follow them.

That disclaimer led to several cries of 'hear, hear' and the tone of the Assembly became more warmly enthusiastic, cheering him when he gave his general impression of the American Churches, albeit from visits limited to the large towns. From these experiences he claimed:

> It is right to say in general, – and I believe my colleagues will concur with me,- that we have received a very favourable impression- a far more favourable impression than I had when I left this country- of the usefulness, and vigour, and efficiency, of the American churches, – of the great amount of Christian good that they are doing, in the midst of many difficulties and discouragements; and I cherish the sincerest respect and esteem for the professional attainments, the personal character, and the ministerial diligence and assiduity, of the great body of those pastors with whom I had the privilege of associating.[1]

Further cheers greeted Cunningham when he spoke of the 'utmost cordiality' and 'utmost kindness' with which the delegation had been received. He wished to inform the Assembly about the geographical spread of Presbyterians, whose thin representation in the north-east was accounted for by the predominance of Congregationalists, whereas the Presbyterian strength in the south was bolstered because 'when the Congregationalists go to the Southern states they become Presbyterians'.

Cunningham assured the Assembly that although the Free Church would have a greater sympathy with the Old and more orthodox Presbyterians who had sometimes been called 'The Scottish party', adhering as they do to 'the principles of the Church of Scotland in its purest form', than the New group, who attached more importance to usefulness than a 'rigid exactness in doctrine', he had found warm support from both camps. He hoped that the support from Old and New for the cause of the Free Church might be a means of uniting them closer. Second to the Presbyterians, he felt, was the support given by the Congregationalists in New England. Although the Baptist and Methodists in New York seemed reluctant at first to come to meetings addressed by the delegation, he claimed that Baptists in Philadelphia and Boston and Methodists in Baltimore received then warmly and some set up collections for the Free Church cause.

'The Church in America', declared Cunningham to much acclaim, 'does not permit its affairs to be regulated by the law of the land and the decisions of the civil courts but by the principles of the word of God and therefore it cordially concurs in all the principles we have been called to maintain'. He continued by informing the Assembly that in addressing these churches, he had explained that it was in adherence to these same principles that they were driven away from a connection with the state and forced to abandon all privileges and emoluments. In America, he explained, it was taken as read that there should be no union between church and state – such a connection being so abhorrent to the churches that they find it hard to appreciate the finer points of conscience which led to the emergence of the Free Church.

Cunningham then instanced two articles in United States publications which had given enthusiastic support to the cause of the Free Church.

One was in the *Princeton Review*, authored by his host at the College, Principal Hodge, in which the author declared 'we wish to have a part in this testimony; we wish to be on their side; to share in their struggles; to participate in their reproach, and bear their burden'. The other was in the journal of the Old School Presbyterians. It declared that the Free Church had demonstrated a key issue of principle on the distinct government of Christ's church as opposed to that of the state. Significantly it went on to assert that the clear 'exhibition of this truth among our churches by the Scottish delegates, will be a means of spiritual good, for which all our contributions will be a most inadequate compensation'. Even if the churches in America were to increase contributions a hundredfold, the author claimed that they would still be debtors to the Free Church for reminding them of the tradition of Knox and Melville and 'the difference between believing that Christ is King and believing that the King is head of the Church'.[2]

The article had, its author proclaimed, two objectives. One was to inform Presbyterians about the significance of the Free Church stand. Secondly, it was to 'minister what little we could to aid the cause of the Scottish delegation to this country'. It recognised that 'a few thousand dollars' would in no way determine the success or failure of the Free Church but 'to be hostile or to be indifferent, would be a sore calamity'.

Moved as he was by reading that declaration of support, William Cunningham told the Assembly that if nothing else had resulted from the trip than to inform the American churches of the Free Church position, the objectives had been secured. He then turned to the funds collected, which he felt represented liberal generosity; although he recognised that some might be disappointed in the figure. So far £9,000 had been contributed with more expected from the Assembly at Kentucky attended by Chalmers and Lewis. He expected another £1,000 to come from Dr Burns's visit to Canada. He then personalised some of the donations.

A key supporter, and one who gave £3,000, was a friend of Thomas Chalmers and a prominent New York business man and philanthropist, James Lennox. Lennox had contributed to theological education in Princeton and elsewhere and he was particularly interested in the overseas mission of the Free Church – his first contribution was to the church's India Mission. Cunningham gave free and florid testimony to Lennox as 'a most intelligent and accomplished Christian gentleman'.

He then informed the Assembly about 'ordinary Scots' and the support from them. He told them of an octogenarian native of Moffat who had walked three miles to shake hands with him and a gardener who contributed a few shillings because he was plagued by the thought of his countrymen having to worship in the open air. The sufferings of Free Church congregations had, said Cunningham, evoked huge sympathy and in one place there was a proposal to bring 700 congregations over to America.

The case of Janet Fraser, a member of the Secession Church, not the Free Church, who had been persecuted by her 'neighbour' (and landlord) the Duke of Buccleuch because of her refusal to worship in the Kirk, had become a cause célèbre. Cunningham held a pair of spectacles given to him for Janet and told of a similar gift of a gold ring entrusted to Robert Burns and communion vessels for her church. Towards the end of his speech Cunningham drew laughter from the Assembly when he quoted the American view that 'these Dukes of yours must be great fools' for thinking they could defeat the Free Church. He told of the approval for the contention that 'Janet Fraser is a far more noble person than the Duke of Buccleuch'.

Henry Ferguson was then invited to address the Assembly. He was fairly brief but couldn't avoid again using the name of Janet Fraser to evoke laughter and applause, detailing the books to be forwarded to her and further gifts of two gold rings. In one village where he had related her story in broad Scots the women of the community had contributed 15 dollars to be given to Janet. He spoke of a dying woman in the south who had feared that she would not meet the delegation but made a donation through a friend, saying that when the delegates arrived she would 'be with John Knox and the rest of the Scottish Reformers'. Ferguson then sat down 'amid great applause'.[3]

Adulation and Omission

Not once was the issue of slavery even alluded to in either speeches. After Henry Ferguson had resumed his seat, Dr Robert Gordon, minister of the Free Church on Edinburgh's High Street rose to his feet to express the Assembly's warm thanks to God and also thanks to William Cunningham for all his labours. Without underestimating the liberality of the American churches, Gordon felt that the communication of Free Church principles had been the crucial task of the delegation. In this, he was convinced, William Cunningham had been an excellent advocate. He proposed that the Assembly congratulate William Cunningham on a safe return and thank him for all that he had done to expound and spread those principles, not forgetting 'the excellent friend who last addressed us'.

After the motion had been agreed by the Assembly, the Moderator, Henry Grey, addressed Cunningham and told him of the high estimation in which he was held by the Assembly, the gratitude they all felt for his zeal, and devotion, his willingness to undertake such a journey on behalf of the church, and the success of his labours. Amidst this peon of praise the Moderator stated that the Assembly were 'happy to include in our vote of thanks our respected friend Mr Ferguson'.

The Moderator continued by looking at the Presbyterian Church in America – the largest Presbyterian Church in the world, he emphasised – with 'esteem and gratitude'. Discordant issues could not entirely be swept under the carpet but he chose to concentrate on the denominational differences with the Baptists and Congregationalists, as well as the Old and New Presbyterians. 'We are happy to understand' he said optimistically, 'that their controversies are dying away and that a greater and more comprehensive charity begins to prevail'. The visit by the delegates had, he was certain, provided a rallying point. The sympathy for the Free Church had been able to unite churches that had otherwise been divided and in addition to the gifts brought home to Scotland from the exchange, the Free Church delegation had been able to be a blessing to those they had visited. 'A practical demonstration of Christian principle, seen from a distance, and therefore exempt from the distorting or decomposing influence of party feeling or rivalry' could not, he argued, fail to reconcile.

Then followed a peroration that made even higher claims for the success of the delegation. The visit, continued Grey, had not only 'laid the foundation of a friendly correspondence that will not soon be dropped' but more significantly,

> May even contribute, in no small degree, to the preservation of peace, and of all the relations of friendship, between two great nations, united in respect of their origin, their language, their religion, – nations that ought to "love as brethren," but will never be brought to obey that royal law until they be thoroughly imbued with the spirit of the gospel, and find in

its sacred influence that perfect uniting bond that can never be broken,- that "bond of perfectness" which joins in one, nations the most remote, ranks the furthest asunder, the rich and poor, the master and servant, the freeman and the slave.[4]

Thus for the first time at the Assembly was slavery was given a passing mention and only in what Assembly members would recognise as a biblical weaving together of Paul's letter to the Church in Corinth and the Epistle to the Hebrews. It could scarcely be more oblique and would have caused little disquiet from the most hardened of slave-owners in Charleston, such a key centre of support for the Free Church. At one level they would have been horrified at the full implication of St. Paul's instruction that in Christ all earthly divisions fall away. But at another, the idea of a 'bond of perfectness' between master and servant fitted the mythology that the Southern way of life was a perfect ordering of things under God and one that was only challenged by the ungodly and the rabble-rousers.

It is more than likely that Grey's intention in linking the delegation's work with the fostering of peace between Great Britain and America, was a subtle dig at the British government, whose actions had forced all at the Assembly to leave the Church of Scotland. Even half-a-century since the American colonies broke away from the motherland, relationships between the two nations were still stormy. The sympathy for, and identification with, the freedom and independence that were mantras for the white citizens of the United States, found an easy echo in this new Church in Scotland who identified with those rights and struggles.

Nothing from the chair and no speech from the floor of the Assembly gave a hint of recognition to the issue that would have to be raised on Friday next, 24 May. The issue of the American churches' attitude to slavery was not going to blight the reception of that report. It was of course an issue unavoidably there in the minds of any commissioners who had even a brief acquaintance with the United States. But it was not to be mentioned. It was the elephant in the room which everyone could see but whose presence no one was prepared to acknowledge.

The Glasgow Emancipation Society stirs the pot and Humble Overtures break the silence

Before the Free Church delegation visited America, the Glasgow Emancipation Society was urging churches in Scotland to break fellowship with the American churches who admitted slave-owners to their membership. Rev. George Jeffrey of the United Secession Church, at a public meeting in Glasgow on 17 August 1843 moved that no ministers from the United States 'who are not thorough advocates of the anti-slavery cause' should be admitted to pulpits in Scotland. [5]

The Glasgow Emancipation Society had been founded in 1833 in the wake of the Act abolishing slavery in the British Empire and it immediately turned to the task of assisting American abolitionists. Its first full meeting had been held in the Congregational Church in the city whose minister was the veteran abolitionist, Dr Ralph Wardlaw, credited with inspiring the young David Livingstone from Blantyre with anti-slavery sermons and lectures. One of its first Secretaries was William Smeal, a Quaker merchant, whose family were to fill key positions in the Glasgow and Edinburgh anti-slavery societies. The other was John Murray, a collector of customs, who had personal experience of the West Indies and had been active in the latter stages of the British campaign. Their leadership was to ensure a more radical and uncompromising stance than their counterparts in the capital. The Society under them maintained a loyalty to William Lloyd Garrison's American Anti-Slavery Society. Yet it had been the more cautious American and Foreign Anti-Slavery Society run by the Tappan brothers, who had first pled with the Free Church delegates not to accept money from the south.

The Glasgow Emancipation Society now drew leading sup-porters not only from other parts of Scotland but from all over the world. The first Secretary was Daniel O'Connell, the radical Irish parliamentarian. James McCune Smith, an African American medical student at Glasgow University, was a founder member of the Committee. Until the abandonment of the Apprenticeship Scheme in 1838 much of the Society's attention was given to getting rid of this new form of slavery, which had been part of the compromise offered to the sugar planters in the West Indies. Having achieved that, their attention was turned to urging diplomatic pressure on nations such as Brazil, where slavery was rife and where trading links with Britain were strong. Increasingly, the Society gave priority support to the fragile and vulnerable abolition movement in the United States.

The guest speaker at that public meeting in August 1843 was Henry C. Wright, a hat maker from New York, who had been ordained in the Congregational church and was now one of the anti-slavery lecturers in the United States. Wright was to spend five years in Europe between 1842 and 1847. He had fallen out with the American Anti-Slavery Society who saw him as too radical in his disdain for any authority. That August evening in Glasgow he was as uncompromising as ever.

The title of Henry Wright's lecture was *'The American Churches – the bulwarks of American Slavery'*. After making his case out to show how Christianity was used to accept, even justify slavery, the Society invited him to move the first resolution. Wright's preface ran:

> Whereas the Christian scriptures enjoins it on the followers of Christ to 'withdraw from every brother that walketh disorderly' and 'to have no fellowship with the unfruitful works of darkness' and whereas God has denounced his sore judgements on all who, when they see a thief, consent with him who are partakers with adulterers, and whereas both branches of the Presbyterian Church in the United States, together with the leading denominations of that country do fellowship with the unfruitful works of darkness and become partakers in theft and robbery by admitting slaveholders to their communion and pulpits as Christians and Christian ministers. . ..

He then proposed, and the Society resolved unanimously to approve, the suggestion made by a minister in Ohio that true abolitionists should withdraw from the pro-slavery organisations of that country 'lest by continuing in them they help to rivet the chain of the slaves by throwing over the foul system of slavery the sanctions of Christianity'. George Jeffrey's motion on the denial of pulpits to any except abolitionists from the United States was carried. It was nothing short of calling for a ban on fellowship with American Presbyterians before the Free Church delegation had even sailed.[6]

It is no surprise therefore to find seven months later a strong and uncompromising challenge from the Glasgow Emancipation Society to the Free Church. On 14 March 1844, George Jeffrey moved the 'regret' of the Society that 'the Free Church of Scotland or any evangelical church' should accept money from church members known to be slave-holders. The meeting then agreed to 'affectionately and earnestly' call on office-bearers and members of the Free Church to:

> Acquit themselves as becomes Christians and Scotchmen in regard to pecuniary contributions from American Slaveholders *and in particular, the contributions sent them from Charleston, South Carolina* (underlined in the minute book) not to accept of such but to refuse and send them back to the donors, accompanied with a faithful and plain dealing testimony to the American Churches against slavery'. [7]

It was agreed at that meeting to send copies of this to the members

of the Free Church Presbytery of Glasgow, to every Presbytery in
Scotland and to the Moderator of the General Assembly, Dr Henry
Grey. On 25 May Grey acknowledged the correspondence but stated
that he could not put this to the Assembly because 'the subject
would come to the Assembly by 'overture' from two Synods, those
of Clydesdale and Ayr, and Lothian and Tweeddale. [8]

By this time press publicity had reached a wider audience
than the Free Church on the resolutions agreed by the Glasgow
Emancipation Society. The letter from the American and Foreign
Anti-Slavery Society to the delegates of the Free Church and the
issue of fellowship with, and acceptance of help from, churches
conniving with slavery was also public knowledge. Any hopes of
the issue being buried within the Church's courts were by this time
a forlorn hope.

Dr Candlish takes the reins

Immediately after the Moderator had received delegates from the
newly independent Presbyterian Church of England and expressed
the hope of 'a mutual and frequent communication', the Assembly
called for Overtures on Slavery in America. Within the proceedings
of Presbyterian Church Assemblies the lower court of Synod,
representing Presbyteries, could send what were termed 'Overtures'
to the General Assembly for consideration. On 8 May 1844, the
Synod in whose area the Assembly was meeting, sent the following
to the commissioners gathered in Edinburgh:

It is humbly overtured by the Synod of Lothian and Tweeddale
to the venerable General Assembly, that they take into their
serious consideration the propriety of addressing, in a friendly
and brotherly spirit, the Presbyterian and other churches in
the United States of America, on the continuance of slavery in
that country, and the countenance alleged to be given to it by
professing Christians and religious communities.

Alongside the Synod, which included the capital, was another overture
from the largest Presbyterian Synod in the world – that of Clydesdale
and Ayr. This included the city of Glasgow, one that had not long
since played a significant financial part in the slave-trade and slavery
and also in the campaign to abolish both of these. Their Overture
preceded the one from the east by about three weeks, called for 'an
earnest remonstrance in reference to the sin of slavery' and requested
the appointment of a Committee to report to the Commission of
Assembly (a body drawn from the General Assembly delegates).[9]

Dr Robert Candlish

The person to respond to the Overtures was Dr Robert Candlish, who, with Chalmers and Cunningham, was already seen as a major figure in the Free Church. As a student of theology in Glasgow he had been strongly influenced by Thomas Chalmers. In 1834, at the age of twenty-eight, Candlish had been called to be minister of the prestigious church of St. George's in Edinburgh, his native city. Such was the effectiveness of his ministry that Princeton awarded him a Doctorate in 1841. He had been preferred by St. George's at the last minute to William Cunningham with whom he was to share many of the ups and downs of leadership in the Free Church. The two men were very different in temperament and for some years were estranged from each other over approaches to theological education. Cunningham earlier claimed that he would attempt to keep 'that Moderate' (Candlish) out of the pulpit.

Robert Candlish made an immediate appeal for caution in response to the Overtures. Given the report earlier that week of the present or potential relationship between the Presbyterian 'and other churches' in America and what he termed 'the Free Protesting Church of Scotland', this was for him, a delicate situation. Candlish admitted and even approved of 'the vehement indignation which we are apt to feel whenever slavery is contemplated'. He could hardly do less, given the strength and passion of the attack on West Indian slavery and the radical call for its immediate abolition, made from his pulpit by his predecessor but one in St. George's, Dr Andrew Thomson. He himself had already been involved in anti-slavery protests and undoubtedly felt strongly on the issue. But he was also careful to avoid any possible friction within the fragile and fledgling body that was the Free Church of Scotland. He asked the Assembly to consider what method might be best employed in furthering abolition.

A first step towards this, argued Candlish, was to enquire how the Free Church could best improve communications with the American churches. 'I would desire' he continued, 'to abstain on this occasion from pronouncing any judgement as to what the American churches have been doing, or ought to do, in this matter; for to a large extent, as a church, we are ignorant on the whole subject'. It was of course a tactical move to avoid upsetting the American Presbyterians. There would be plenty of evidence on the American churches way of approaching slavery that would be available from members of the delegation not yet home – the same day that the overtures were discussed, William Chalmers and George Lewis had heard 'with dismay' the way in which the General Assembly of the Presbyterian Church dealt with the issue of slavery at their meeting in Kentucky. To various cries of approval, Candlish suggested that the influence of the churches in America had been good for the Free Church, therefore there might be an opportunity for the Free Church in future to exert an influence for good in return. But not just now.

Candlish proposed what so many in church assemblies had done before to avoid immediate decisions – that a Committee be set up to investigate the matter and report to the Commission of Assembly; a body selected from the commissioners to that year's Assembly which met between the annual gatherings and had powers of decision. He repeated his assertion that the church was ignorant of the facts and pled that 'the excitement which this topic is fitted to produce in the mind of every many of generous or Christian feeling' should give way to calm and deliberate consideration. Finally he suggested that Cunningham might aid them in their task of considering the subject 'in a spirit of friendship to the churches in America, and yet in a spirit of faithfulness to the cause remitted to it'. The proposal was agreed and the Committee was appointed, with Candlish as its Convenor.

Before the debate was closed, however, William Cunningham made another short speech that would set the tone for the Committee and would prove to be quite significant in driving a wedge between the Free Church and the supporters of abolition. 'I will not enter on any discussion of the subject', he began, and then proceeded to do so. He warned of unspecified difficulties faced by the American churches in taking action themselves on slavery. 'We do not need to modify the feelings prevailing in this country of abhorrence against the system of slavery', he continued, but argued that the usual impressions propagated in this country 'by the party who exclusively claim to themselves the title of abolitionists' might need considerable modification before any specific measures were adopted. Whether Cunningham was referring to the Glasgow Emancipation Society or the American abolitionists in his charge of their exclusive claim on truth is uncertain. Nevertheless his refusal to question the behaviour of the American church in this matter, indicated that there were certain pressures exerted upon him.[10]

Six months before the Free Church Assembly was challenged over slavery in America, a correspondence had begun between student members of the Edinburgh Missionary Association (later to be New College Missionary Society) and students at Princeton. The Association had been founded in the city but was principally based at the University. It provided a focus for those who were zealous about the overseas mission of the churches and received information from missionaries in different parts of the world.

In 1792, the great year of petitions against the slave trade in Britain, a key argument from the churches had been the incompatibility of preaching the gospel of freedom in the continent of Africa, when its people were being enslaved and transported at the behest of Christian nations. This obvious inconsistency was the subject of those early communications between students from Edinburgh and Princeton. On 30 September 1843 a letter from Princeton expressed pleasure at receiving news from the Edinburgh Missionary Association after the foundation of the Free Church of Scotland. The Free Church students had obviously pre-empted their elders, since the Princeton response continued: 'You ask for information respecting slavery amongst us. There is not one of our religious denominations, which, by general rules, excludes slave-holders, or dealers, from the church, so far as we are informed'.[11]

The Committee reports that everyone was against slavery

On 11 September 1844 the Commission of Assembly heard a report drawn up by the Committee appointed less than four months previously. In introducing it, Dr Candlish emphasised that this was an interim piece of work and that the Committee was not yet ready to furnish 'a final and decisive judgement' on the matter raised by the Overtures. He assured the Commission that what he was about to say had the unanimous support of the members of the Committee. No one, he argued, had any doubt that 'slavery in all its forms is to be regarded as a system of oppression which cannot be defended'. Natural reason, justice, 'the tenor and spirit of the divine word', and in particular the gospel, all combined, in the Committee's view, to condemn it.

Candlish echoed the sentiments in a previous century of the historian and Moderate leader of the Church of Scotland, William Robertson, when he claimed that it was due to the influence of Christianity that slavery had been mitigated, discontinued, and abolished in many parts of the world. Therefore, he told the Commission, 'it is with the deepest pain' that every Christian must regard the continuation of slavery in the United States, a country that boasted of equal liberties and equal rights. He would go further, he said, in pointing out that in the provisions made for replenishing slave numbers, the obstacles put in the way of religious education of slaves and the laws protecting the masters, self-evidently, or to his thinking, 'must characterise American slavery as one of the most deplorable forms of that evil, peculiarly [particularly] calling for the exertions of a sound Christian philanthropy in regard to it'.

Nothing in the report so far would have caused anything but satisfaction to the Tappan brothers and their colleagues in the American and Foreign Anti-Slavery Society. Nor would they have baulked at the recognition Candlish gave to British responsibility for a trade and an institution that until very recently was to be found within the British Empire, which of course included pre-independent America. He pointed to the better example set by British abolition and the encouragement that its success would hold for others to follow suit. In that regard, he declared, 'the Committee cannot but consider it the duty of Christian churches, as such, to set themselves against its manifold abuses, and to aim decidedly at its abolition', nor could the Committee conceive of churches sanctioning it without considering their responsibility for 'the calamities which flow from it'.

So far so good. Candlish then turned to qualify his remarks, and the common ground shared by his committee with the abolitionists started to evaporate. The Committee felt, he reported, that it was not appropriate for them to 'decide peremptorily' the particular course of duty to be universally and immediately adopted by the American churches. The Free Church was privy to inadequate and scanty information, it had insufficient communication with the American churches and it was ignorant of the 'motives that may have weight with particular churches'. Moreover, he continued, it would be ill advised if the Committee sought to judge, let alone condemn, the American churches in this matter, bearing in mind the record of British churches, both at home and abroad, who had been far from clear about how they ought to deal with slavery. The committee did not believe that the British churches 'did all that it was their duty to do against the system of slavery', rather the reverse. Later on the report stated that despite that influence of the 'Christian faithfulness of devoted men' in ending British slavery, they were hindered by the 'vacillating and uncertain conduct of not a few of the ministers and churches of Christ'.

In a rather strange twist, the Candlish Committee then stated that they would not 'indicate any disapprobation of the rule or principle on which some of the American churches now act in opposition to that system'. The abolitionists, in analysing that statement were later to say that that was indeed the problem – there did not seem to be any rule or principle which caused the American churches to take action against slavery.

The unease in the Committee, for all its unanimity, was obvious as it appeared to swing between affectionate solidarity and stern reminders to the churches in America of the consequences of participation in 'this evil' (slavery) and its repeated reluctance to 'prescribe' or 'dictate' any form of action. One sentence read 'delay in this case can scarcely be productive of any good', whilst another reaffirmed the idea that the Free Church was in 'ignorance of their circumstances'. The conclusion of the report was that in the light of the above there was 'no reason for interrupting the friendly intercourse so happily begun, and cultivated by reciprocal visits and good offices' (between the Free Church of Scotland and the Presbyterian churches in America) but expressed the hope that a mutually beneficial relationship could be built though 'friendly counsel and sympathy and, if need be, admonition and encouragement'. To this end the Committee solicited the American churches' 'earnest attention to a subject which excites so strong a feeling in the minds of British Christians'.[12]

It was not a document that was to satisfy anyone but the Commission of Assembly to whom they reported, and who agreed that it should be sent to the United States. The abolitionists, with some justification, saw it as ducking the issue and were annoyed that nothing was said or done about the money received from the Southern states. The Glasgow Emancipation Society at a public meeting on 18 November 1844 expressed itself as 'deeply grieved at the indifference of the Free Church'. On the other side some of the Southern leaders who had raised support for the delegation were equally disturbed and angry that the report even contained critical comments on slavery. They too, as we shall see, felt let down. In the next six months, however, the Committee and the Free Church General Assembly, were to be pushed further in this direction, but the damage was already done.

Chapter 3
Chalmers and Smyth – Tensions across the Atlantic.

Our understanding of Christianity is that it deals not with civil or political institutions but that it deals with persons and with ecclesiastical institutions, and that the objects of these last is to operate directly and proximately with the most wholesome effect on the consciences and characters of persons
Dr. Thomas Chalmers, letter to *The Witness*, May 1844

A blast from the deep South

On 24 May 1844, the day that the Free Church Assembly heard the two Overtures on slavery, Dr Thomas Smyth, minister of Second Presbyterian Church in Charleston, South Carolina, wrote to his friend Dr Thomas Chalmers. He enclosed a sum of £332.10.10 in addition to an amount already forwarded 'in connection with the labours of Mr Lewis and Mr Ferguson'. He estimated this to be a large sum, considering that the portion of the population in the city who 'sympathised with Presbyterianism' was comparatively small. Smyth said that he had never seen such interest in any cause and such liberality, some from those who gave far beyond their means. This was all the more remarkable because, he maintained, 'the sympathy of some part of this body [friends of Presbyterianism] was studiously alienated by the opposition of your own clergymen here and other Scotchman'. Smyth continued:

> And now, my dear Sir, judge of the pain and grief with which we have received accounts of certain proceedings in Glasgow and Edinburgh in which representatives of the Free Church took part and where there is a glaring want of all courtesy, not to say Christian charity. The course pursued by Dr. Candlish, for whom I have cherished such a warm and enthusiastic admiration, and the sentiments ascribed to him have given me *much* distress. Some very respectable men here and Scotchman among the rest, have expressed great regret at the declaration of his *intended* proceedings. Certain it is that we would never

have been forward to tender our Christian sympathy and assistance, had we conceived the possibility of having our gifts reciprocated by anathemas and abuse. Judged by every mark and evidence of true faith and piety, there are many among us whom God has called by his grace and spirit. Christians here read and study their bibles and pray for wisdom properly to understand God's will and their duty. And it is their desire to act in accordance with what they believe to be required of them by him to whom all judgement belongeth and to whom they must give their final account. They cannot but think that it is going beyond their province and contrary to that 'charity which hopeth all things and beareth all things', when Christians abroad undertake to sit in judgement upon us and, without an opportunity of examining into the circumstances of our case, pronounce upon us a sentence of excommunication from the one great brotherhood of Christianity. And it does seem to me much inconsistent with that proclamation of goodwill and confraternity which the Free Church has made to Christians of every evangelical denomination, not withstanding their manifest aberrations from the polity or doctrines of the Bible. On some points – were she now to refuse the right hand of fellowship, while she protested if needs be against those institutions which she could not but regard as inconsistent with the *spirit* - for no man can say they are within the *letter*-of the gospel.[1]

Of course there were inaccuracies in these charges. As we have seen, the Overtures brought from the two Synods simply asked the Assembly to consider a brotherly communication to the American churches. There was at no time a suggestion that they should 'pronounce a sentence of excommunication'. The attack on Robert Candlish for 'anathemas and abuse' was incredible considering his unwillingness in the Assembly to pass any judgement, or offer even advice on what the American churches might do. Candlish did of course term slavery 'a great iniquity' and said that they all contemplated it with 'vehement indignation'. He was reputed to have participated earlier that year in protests over the death sentence imposed on John L. Brown in South Carolina, who had assisted a slave to escape.[2] This was probably enough to fire the wrath of a church leader in Charleston, one of the centres of the slave-holding South.

There was, however, another reason and one which explains the hurt rather than anger in the letter. Smyth was a passionate supporter of the Free Church, a passion not shared by all churchmen in the city. He had managed, with a bit of a struggle, to secure pulpits for George Lewis and in 1844 a pamphlet of his had been published in New York and London with the lengthy title *The Exodus of the Church of Scotland and the Claims of the Free Church to the Sympathy and Assistance of American Christians.* After all this, he obviously felt a sense of betrayal as reports reached him of Scottish abolitionists, reports from some colleagues who were already suspicious of him.

Then there was the Glasgow Emancipation Society. Although many of its leading lights were clergy, few were Free Church ones, but one of the key figures in the society was its Vice-President, the well respected Free Church minister of Renfield Church in Glasgow, Dr Michael Willis.[3] The Glasgow Emancipation Society's close links with the American abolitionists, increasingly with the more radical Garrison wing, made them more than suspect in the South. A typical southerner would correctly deduce that the Glasgow abolitionists sought to destroy their way of life.

However Thomas Smyth was not just a typical southerner. He was born in Belfast in 1808 and was educated there and in London. He emigrated with his parents to the United States in 1830 and trained for the Presbyterian ministry at Princeton, although he came from a Congregationalist background. In 1832 he was called to be supply preacher at Second Presbyterian Church in Charleston where he spent most of his ministry. Smyth was a scholar and a book lover who was awarded an honorary doctorate by Princeton in 1843 and by that time had extensive international and ecumenical contacts. By the standards of the South he was seen to be a theological and political liberal. Smyth strongly promoted lay participation in the leading of worship and saw Presbyterianism as simply a form of church organisation that could be equally well matched by Methodism. Frederick Porcher, a noted Charlestonian, said of Smyth 'He was fond of talking and never let a subject pass him, but his talk was not always to the point. There was a lot of palaver about him'.[4]

On the issue of slavery, Smyth was as regarded with suspicion and even hostility from his contemporaries in the South as he was to be by abolitionists in the North and in Europe. Although he could hardly fail to be a supporter of slavery (he could not otherwise have survived a ministry in the South) he argued strongly for humane conditions for slaves and was especially keen on their religious education. Smyth supported the efforts of the South Carolina minister and plantation owner Rev. Charles Colcock Jones, whom he met in 1835 and with whom he served on a Committee of the Presbyteries of South Carolina and Georgia, charged with the religious instruction of slaves. Smyth himself was a key figure in establishing the Zion Presbyterian Church for slaves in Charleston. He believed that slavery was an evil but that God would 'open the way' for its removal in time. Professor Erskine Clarke of Columbia Seminary, which Smyth helped to found, describes Smyth, with much justification, as a 'moderate of the Old South'.[5] For this he was given a hard time by his neighbours and when he published a book in 1850, *The Unity of the Human Race,* affirming the humanity of black people, he was accused of being an abolitionist.

All this may explain and even justify Smyth's powerful and at times intemperate letter to Thomas Chalmers. He felt that what he had heard threatened the 'moderate' stance which he had adopted. He felt betrayed over his attempts to revise the system and work towards its ending and he wanted his friend to intervene in order to limit, as he saw it, the damage done to the fragile building up of relationships between Southern Presbyterians and the Free Church. Where did Chalmers stand on the issue of slavery?

The cautious abolitionist

In 1814 Thomas Chalmers was the parish minister of Kilmany in Fife. In July of that year he moved successfully in the Presbytery of Cupar that a petition should be sent to Parliament urging that the abolition of the French slave-trade be one of the conditions of the peace treaty in Paris, now that the war between Britain and France had (temporarily, as it turned out) ended. He spoke passionately against the evils of a commerce that had been ended by law in the British Empire seven years previously.[6]

In the 1820s, when he was a minister in Glasgow, Chalmers had frequent contact with several members of the Clapham Sect, the Evangelical Anglicans who were active in many causes of which the chief one was the abolition of slavery. Chalmers knew William Wilberforce, Thomas Clarkson, and Zachary Macaulay, son of a highland manse, who attempted to secure him as Professor of Moral Philosophy in the new University of London before Chalmers accepted a similar chair at the University of Edinburgh. In 1826 Chalmers wrote a small pamphlet at the behest of Thomas Clarkson entitled *A Few Thoughts on the Abolition of Colonial Slavery.*[7]

Even allowing for the fact that the British emancipation campaign was still at an early stage, moving cautiously along the path of 'mitigating' the worst horrors of the institution and looking into the distance for its final abolition, the pamphlet did not sit easily with the

London based campaign. A simple mathematical calculation of the plan the pamphlet set out, revealed that for a slave to emancipate him or herself and the family (for their freedom too had to be purchased by labour) would have taken many decades. It also betrayed a naïve assumption that Southern slave-owners would willingly permit their slaves to have sufficient time off work in order to gain their liberation from the plantation.

It reflected Chalmers's passionate opposition to governmental intervention to support the poor and provide relief, except where (during the Irish famine for example) there was no obvious alternative. Chalmers's own schemes in Glasgow to encourage and enable the poor to raise themselves out of the mire by their own efforts are reflected in this to enable slaves to earn their freedom through extra work. Another reason for the cautious approach might well have been that his late father and older brother had, in company with so many in Scotland, invested money in the business of the slave trade in the 1790s. To be too strongly critical of those involved in slavery could have led to a charge of hypocrisy. [8]

For these reasons, and in contrast to his predecessor in the leadership of the Kirk's evangelical party, Andrew Thomson, Chalmers was not known for passionate advocacy of emancipation.[9] But because his leadership in the church, his scholarship, preaching and brilliant organisational skills had made him the best known Scottish churchman of his time, it was natural that the abolitionists sought to gain his support. A letter was sent to him on 20 December 1843 from Elihu Burritt, the Editorial Correspondent of the New England Anti-Slavery Tract Society. After the introduction and salutations, Burritt came straight to the point. 'The Christians of this land', he said:

> look to you with a sentiment of profound veneration and filial respect. No man in the wide world could exert a more powerful and salutary influence upon our religious community than yourself. Anything from your pen written with special reference to any of the great questions that are now agitating our country, would deeply affect the American mind'. Above all now is slavery. I am compelled to acknowledge that *slavery* as well as freedom is a 'peculiar' institution of America.[10]

The writer continued by assuring Chalmers of how moved many had been by the secession of the Free Church in 'victory over the arrogance of civil power'. They rejoiced that the church had come out of the fire 'with all her gold seven time purified'. But for all the trials of the Free

Church, said Burritt, she should be grateful that she has never had to cope with the 'dark institution of human slavery', whose 'leprous distilments . . . are poisoning the fountains of our peace and moral life'. Worse still, he continued, the constitution of the country had been 'twisted' in its support, and the Bible and the gospel of Jesus likewise suffered distortion. 'Oh Sir', he wrote 'if you could attend one of the General Assemblies of the Presbyterian Church and listen to the cold blooded profanation of God's blessed word'.

Of course George Lewis and William Chalmers were to attend the General Assembly of the Presbyterian Church in Kentucky the following May. When Lewis wrote to Chalmers from Pittsburgh after it, he described total polarisation of the Northern and Southern churches on discussion of slavery. 'The moment that it was announced in the Assembly that there were overtures from the North on slavery', he reported 'a meeting was called at a caucus of Southern members to consider what they had to do . . . great resentment prevailed'. Lewis went on to observe that any raising of the issue led to the Southerners retreating into a defensive position 'having to cut their own way like Hannibal over the Alps and being strengthened by the difficulties and trials'.[11]

Elihu Burritt explained to Chalmers that the anti-slavery movement in America was unpopular, deemed fanatical by many, and that even in the free states the majority of the clergy distance themselves from it. He proposed a series of tracts written by eminent men, including a number from England and Scotland and urged 'a short contribution from your pen' that, he believed would 'stay these outrages upon the attributes of God and the sanctity of the Bible'. He believed that this would 'fence in' God's word from the profanity of those that sought to 'hang it like a millstone to the neck of the slave'. 'If you would graciously contribute a few reflections' he suggested, 'designed to refute the *Bible arguments in support of slavery*, and suggest what the church should do'. He estimated that 500,000 could be printed and distributed in the pews of every evangelical church in the free states.

Thomas Chalmers may have responded to Burritt but he certainly never offered any lines on slavery to the New England Society. Over the winter of 1843–44 he was engaged in an enormous number of tasks for the church as well as lecturing and preaching. The whole financial burden of keeping the Free Church of Scotland afloat had been assumed by him and at sixty-four years of age his health was suffering severe strains. In fact he delayed or omitted a reply to Thomas Smyth for many months. The Charleston minister wrote to

Dr Thomas Chalmers

Chalmers at the end of August 1844 reminding him that 'according to agreement' he should write a reply to the letter from Smyth which had enclosed the money from Charleston, 'as it regards the feelings of our Free Church brethren towards us & the views they entertain as to the necessity or purpose of interfering with the institution of slavery'. Smyth was on a visit to Britain and had obviously had a meeting with Chalmers (and presumably come to the 'agreement' referred to) when he continued:

> The publication of a letter in accordance with the sentiments expressed by you this morning would, I am sure, have a very salutary and happy effect in reversing misapprehension, and satisfying the mind of many whose fears and jealousies have been awakened by false reports. Such a letter will reach me anytime before the first of October in Dublin.[12]

The phrase 'interfering with the institution of slavery' marked clear battle lines, but what was this 'agreement' between them? Professor George Shepperson has pointed out that the disappearance of all but one highly publicised letter to Smyth makes it difficult to understand the full extent of what transpired between them.[13] But clearly Chalmers gave Smyth leave that day to publicise his reply of 25 September.

Chalmers under pressure

'I do not need to assure you', Chalmers began, 'how little I sympathise with those – because slavery happens to prevail in the Southern States of America – would unchristianise that whole region' and continued:

> And who even carry their extravagance so far as to affirm, so long as it subsists, no fellowship or interchange of good offices should take place with its churches or its ministers. As a friend to the universal virtue and liberty of mankind, I rejoice in the prospect of those days when slavery shall be banished from the face of the earth; but most assuredly the wholesale style of excommunication, contended for by some, is not the way to hasten forward this blissful consummation.[14]

Chalmers continued by expressing the hope of a commencement towards emancipation in America and harked back twenty-five years when, after reading Humboldt's travels in South America, he had formulated the little pamphlet for Clarkston. 'I have not been able to engage in any sort of public business since I had the pleasure of meeting with you' he continued, 'but I observe that in our Assembly's Commission, a few weeks back, the subject of American slavery was entertained. I do hope that the Resolutions which they have adopted will prove satisfactory'. The letter ended with fulsome appreciation of their friendship and the hope that Free Church ministers will 'ever entertain a grateful sense of your able and disinterested service'.

Although the letter was to some extent a pouring of oil over troubled waters, neither it nor certainly the report adopted by the Commission of Assembly, was to prove satisfactory. For the Southern churchmen any critical word on slavery from outside (they had already driven out those who criticised it from inside) was unacceptable, in however friendly and brotherly terms it was couched. For Smyth himself, relationships with the Free Church could never be the same again – a sacred taboo had been breached, however much his friend's soothing words were aimed to heal it. As for Chalmers, he was caught between two stools. He could hardly endorse slavery in America or pretend that it was an acceptable alternative system. On the other hand, the piety, order, and patterned way of life of the old South would have been attractive values to him. He found himself committed to defend the Commission of Assembly's position, although what he had written to Smyth reflected a more conservative position than that modest resolution. Exhausted with the effort and strain of the last year, he now found himself under challenge in his own city from the Edinburgh Emancipation Society. On 4 December 1844 Mr Edward Cruikshank wrote to him in these terms:

At a meeting of the Committee of the Edinburgh Emancipation Society held today, there was laid before the Committee a printed letter proporting to be a copy of one addressed by you to Revd Dr Thomas Smyth of Charleston. The Committee are informed that this letter is receiving a most extensive circulation in the United States, and there is little doubt that it will find its way into the newspapers of this country. The Committee however do not feel themselves warranted in assuming, without further information, that the letter is authentic, and it will afford them much satisfaction to have authority from you for making known that it is not the case, and thus counter-acting in some measure the prejudicial effect on the anti-slavery cause which they consider the circulation of the letter is calculated to produce. By direction of the committee I therefore enclose a copy, and respectfully request that, at your earliest convenience, you will inform us whether the letter, as thus given, has emanated from you.

We are, Revd Sir, with great respect, yours very sincerely[15]
Chalmers replied obliquely to The Edinburgh Emancipation Society
and only in May 1845. He may have acknowledged the letter earlier
but it is clear from his memoirs that he considered the best way of
answering this and other charges was by a lengthy piece offered as a
letter to *The Witness*, the Free Church paper, edited by the redoubtable
Hugh Millar, highland stonemason and author. It was also perhaps
to serve as a response to Lewis Tappan of the American and Foreign
Anti-Slavery Society, under whose auspices the letter had gone to
the delegation over a year previously. Tappan had reacted strongly
to the commendation of Smyth by Chalmers, commenting:

> Its tendency is to put down what we have been attempting for
> 10 years to build up. Such a letter as this proceeding from the
> pen of one whose writings are exerting a great influence in this
> country will do more injury than all the good that will be done
> by his publications in past years.[16]

A careful compromise in *The Witness*

In his letter to *The Witness*, Chalmers acknowledged the charge some
months ago that he had given an 'inadequate deliverance' on the
evils of slavery. He had hoped, he said, that he would have had the
opportunity of sharing in discussion of the issue at the next meeting
of the General Assembly (May 1845), 'but as that expectation will not
now be realised', he requested the opportunity to make his position
clear in the newspaper. Why at this stage it would have been seen as
impossible for him to speak at the Assembly is unclear. There was
no agreed prohibition on discussion of the Candlish Committee's
report, given as an interim one to the Commission of Assembly in
September. It may be that he felt the need to concentrate on the huge
tasks of sustaining the church financially and establishing the new
centre for theological training of Free Church ministers. Slavery in
America would have been a distraction for which he had little time
or energy.

The first point that he wished to make was that 'slavery, like
war, is a great evil'. Any person of enlightenment and humanity,
he believed, would seek the abolition of slavery, and war, from
the earth and support the best means of achieving this. 'Yet', he
maintained, 'destructive and demoralising as both are, and inimical
as Christianity is to all violence, and to all vice, it follows not that there
may not be a Christian soldier, and neither does it follow that there
may not be a Christian slave-holder'. Presumably he would not have

argued the same way over the keeper of a brothel or those who made
their profession in other forms of 'vice', but he continued to assert
that even when a person was engaged in a pursuit that is inimical to
Christianity, it could not be argued that this was incompatible with
their personal Christianity.

It was his second point which caused the greatest reaction
from abolitionists. Chalmers sought to expand on what he saw
as a necessary distinction between 'the character of a system and
the character of the persons whom circumstances have implicated
therein'. 'The system of slavery we rightly recoil from', he said, 'and
charge it with atrocities and evils, often the most hideous and the
most appalling, which have either affected or deformed our species'.
Yet despite this, he continued, we could not say of everyone born
within that system, accustomed to its horrors, 'who by inheritance
is himself an owner of slaves', that unless he renounces his property
and all that belongs to him (slaves being seen as property) 'unless
that surrender is made, he therefore is not a Christian and should be
treated as an outcast from all the distinctions or the privileges of a
Christian society'.

Chalmers then went on to attack what he saw as the hypocrisy
of 'zealous abolitionists' who, if they were placed in the situation
of being slave-holders would do exactly the same and profit from
the system. There were, he maintained, various lines of 'procedure
and policy' with which people could join in seeking the abolition
of slavery. However, in his view 'the most unjustifiable . . . , the
most unwise and least effectual of these, were to pass a wholesale
anathema, by which to unchristianise, or to pass a general sense of
excommunication on slave-holders'.

In his third point, Chalmers conceded that slavery had a corrupting
effect and that there might well be 'inhuman, licentious, barbarous
and brutalised men' in the slave-holding states, but he could not agree
that the state of slave-holding necessarily resulted in these vices. The
vices that frequently result from slavery might, he thought, call for
frequent church discipline in slave-holding congregations. There was
for him a need to debar from the communion table and from Christian
fellowship, those who are listed by the Apostle Paul as, 'a fornicator,
or covetous, or an idolator, or a railor, or a drunkard or an extortioner'.
All these, for Chalmers, were sufficient to debar someone from the
privileges of Christian membership. The grounds of being a slave-
holder alone were not sufficient. 'Let every man' he wrote:

Be he slave-holder or not, be cast out from the brotherhood
of the Christian ordinances, who falls into any of the vices

that are here enumerated; and let the brotherhood of every
church be disowned which is found to tolerate these vices in
its members be they high or low.

Chalmers maintained that any church that failed to discipline its
members for the vices listed and indeed to debar them whilst they
persisted in sin, 'should be treated as an outcast by other churches'.
Even if the General Assembly of the American Presbyterian Church
should collude with this, he hoped that the only correspondence that
the Free Church of Scotland would consent to hold with that church
was 'grave and solemn remonstrance because of the dishonour
done by them [the American church] to our common Lord'. 'Our
understanding of Christianity' he said,

Is that it deals not with civil or political institutions, but that it
deals with persons and with ecclesiastical institutions, and that
the objects of these last is to operate directly and proximately
with the most wholesome effect on the consciences and
characters of persons.

Chalmers expressed confidence that the Free Church would not
deviate from principle but was anxious that she should not be
forced 'by clamour of any sort' to what he described as 'outrun her
convictions', and adopt a policy for which he saw no authority in
scripture or in the history and practice of the early church. He then
turned to the abolitionists, challenging them to detail instances in
America of church members whose lives were characterised by
'concubinage, or their cruelty, or the gross violence and villainy of
any sort' which can be proved. This he saw as a more effective method
to 'augment the moral force of that opposition to slavery' than
enforcing a new principle and requiring a new practice to recognise
slave-holding as a 'sort of ecclesiastical felony'. He was convinced
that if moral standards were rigorously applied to individuals, the
system of slavery would be undermined, whereas the abolitionists'
demands for slave-holding per se as a ground for discipline, would
in fact strength the system.

Strangely, he argued that there should be one exception to this.
Just as the Free Church of Scotland forbad its ministers to hold any
secular trade or employment 'lest it should secularise them', so
he argued that ministers of the American church, whilst not being
forbidden to hold slaves as domestic servants, should be debarred
from being masters of slaves for profit, 'lest it should brutalise them'.

In the final sections of the letter, Chalmers addressed himself to
the issue raised by the abolitionists to the delegation. He referred
to the recent report of the American Board of Commissioners

for Foreign Missions in which there was an article on Memorials on Slavery put before the Board. The memorialists (petitioners) condemned American slavery as 'a system of oppression most unjust and grievous' (a statement with which Chalmers believed the Free Church of Scotland would wholly agree). The memorial continued with a request that the Board should instruct all their missionaries and agents to bear constant witness to American slavery as a sin and grossly at variance with the gospel they are commissioned to preach. They then asked the Board to refuse any money 'contributed by slave-holders or any of the avails of slave labour' and to call for the immediate abolition of slavery.

Chalmers commended the Board for resisting these requests, on several grounds. The duty of propagating the gospel in 'heathen lands' was an object in itself and needed to be pursued single mindedly. To depart from it, they argued, would be to defeat the ends of 'converting the heathen'. The Board presumed that monies contributed by slave-holders was obtained 'in a proper manner' and 'contributed from right motives', and so must be accepted. The American Board had always declared its total disapproval of slavery and would have 'no connection or sympathy with it' praying for its removal but disclaiming any proper action on it to be within their province. This for Chalmers was the position in which the Free Church of Scotland saw itself. He ended the letter with a catalogue of the horrors of slavery – the application of the whip to human beings, the separation of families, the denial of an education, the traffic in human beings. 'There is' he said 'no need of exaggeration' by those who seek to end slavery, but simply exposure of the truth. With an increasing number of Christians and philanthropists working in opposition to slavery he was confident that this would have its effect on the American Government speedily to do what the British government pioneered 'in putting down slavery by law'.[17]

It seems that Thomas Chalmers was somewhat panicked into setting out his, and by implication the Free Church's, justification for what they did and did not do through their delegation to America. The robust denunciation in principle of slavery and the recitation of some of its horrors was the very least that any churchmen could credibly make in a British, let alone Scottish, context. However it cannot have pleased Thomas Smyth any more than it could have fulfilled the request from Elihu Burritt for a theological and biblical analysis. His attempts to separate the vices detailed by Paul the Apostle from a practice that he was forced to characterise as sin and iniquity, was something that would be taken up with good effect by his critics.

For the man who in earlier times spoke of the 'Godly Common-wealth' and drew on the prophetic traditions of his faith to limit the relevance of Christianity to the personal, and seemingly leave the corporate ethic on the side, this was a theological position that would have called for strong criticism if espoused by his students. When he used the American Board of Missions's justification for accepting slave-holders' money on the grounds that there was no reason to think that it was dishonestly earned, it simply opened the floodgates for the public parodies and lampoons on the Free Church's acceptance of similar funds, that would run for the next two years.

Two weeks before Chalmers submitted that piece to *The Witness* Smyth wrote warmly to him with concern about the way his friend had been 'subjected to such intolerance' following the publication of the September letter and commending Cunningham for his 'very able and candid review' (the Assembly speech that didn't mention slavery). Thomas Smyth's admiration for Chalmers was little short of worship. After Thomas Chalmers's death in 1847 an extensive pamphlet was printed in Charleston under Smyth's name in which he commended Chalmers's 'breadth of soul and comprehensiveness of spirit' and his 'noble vindication of this country and especially of the Southern States, against the furious fanaticism of popular and ecclesiastical abolition outcry'. By contrast to what Smyth described as the British mind on American slavery being 'enveloped in the mists of ignorant prejudice and national pride', the mind of Chalmers was, for Smyth, 'enabled to send its penetrating glance and to form, to a great extent, a correct Christian and philosophical estimate of this grave question'.[18] In his April 1844 letter to Chalmers, Smyth expressed the hope that Christians could get on with preaching the gospel 'unfettered by prejudice executed by external influence'. It was well past that stage. Slavery could not be swept under the carpet.

Chapter 4
Keeping a Lid on the Volcano

*Have we separated ourselves from our Moderate brethren to form
alliance with man-stealers? Do we remove from us a brother that
walketh disorderly – a drunkard, a fornicator – an adulterer, to unite
ourselves with man-stealers, sellers of their own offspring, stained
with the blood of innocents, leprous with sin?*

Rev. Henry Grey, Moderator of the Free Church
General Assembly, 13 March 1845

The Glasgow Abolitionists enter the fray again

Although there were many rumblings about the support received
by the Free Church from a church that kept slave-holders in its
membership, 1845 was to see the issue largely ignored in Scotland,
apart from the activities of two groups. One was the Glasgow
Emancipation Society, with their close contacts with American
abolitionists who sought to stir up feelings about the actions of
the Free Church. The other was the leadership of the Free Church,
headed by Drs Cunningham and Candlish, intent on dousing fires
and maintaining the position that whilst they zealously deplored
American slavery, that did not warrant returning the money, still
less breaking ties with the American churches.

At a committee meeting of the Glasgow Emancipation Society
on 1 July 1844, the Secretaries reported that they had written to the
Moderator of the Free Church General Assembly enquiring about
the result of the Overtures that had been sent to the Assembly.
Henry Grey had replied on 21 June, informing the Committee that
the issue had been raised by, he thought, two or three Presbyteries,
but it was felt to be 'attended with difficulties' and had been
referred to a Committee. He continued by assuring the Society
that his brethren and he personally considered 'the existence of
slavery among professing Christians in the United States the most
melancholy and dishonouring aspect of their social state and above
all their religious profession'. The relevant question for him was
what kind of 'interference' might contribute to its overthrowal. The

Committee noted this, but clearly the matter was not, as far as they were concerned, laid to rest.

They then turned to the possibility of questioning Dr Robert Burns, a member of the delegation and described by the Society as 'our old esteemed coadjutor in the anti-slavery cause'. Clearly Burns was still seen as a valued supporter of the Society since the Committee asked that 'the utmost kindness and courtesy' should be shown to him. It was decided to ask Dr Michael Willis, still highly regarded in the Free Church, to put relevant questions to Dr Burns regarding the acceptance of slave-holders' money.[1]

On 1 August the Committee met again before the Annual Meeting of the Society. Two members had gone to a lecture given by Dr Burns. They had considered that it would be damaging to question him publicly, but had met him afterwards and reported that they were satisfied that his 'sentiments on the great question of abolition were perfectly sound'. However, they could not avoid regretting that he and his colleagues, when in America, had not 'borne a more firm and decided testimony against the crying iniquity of that country, and lifted up their voice in [sic] behalf of bleeding humanity'.[2]

That evening at the Annual Meeting, Robert Burns was introduced to the members of the Society with 'great admiration' for his 'eminent services in the cause'. Clearly Burns felt that he needed to justify the position of the Free Church delegation and he proceeded to do so in a debate that broke the unanimity of the Society's previous strictures on how to deal with slavery.

He began with an emotional affirmation of his support for the 'great principles for which you have so long and so honourably contended', and spoke of the joy he shared in Glasgow about the success of final abolition in the colonies finally in 1838. Burns wished to move the adoption of the Annual Report but had to enter his dissent over its remarks on the delegation. He acknowledged that he might have consulted with the Society before going to America and that neither he, nor his colleague Dr Cunningham had realised then that the American churches were so closely linked with slavery. But he affirmed that the Society's condemnation was 'too sweeping' since there were four Presbyterian churches who 'act on the principle of having no fellowship with those who hold human property'.

Robert Burns went on to raise the issue of Northern implication with slavery, particularly the economic ties with cotton. If Britain were to do what many advocated in the days of West Indian slavery, only buy sugar from 'free' sources, then that might, he said, have made a difference. A strong element in America, he claimed, was sensitive towards any 'interference' from Britain and the way in which slavery was seen as a civil institution, in which a church, separated from the State, should not have any business. There was also their refuge in the claim that there was no positive condemnation of slavery in scripture. Burns specifically disassociated himself with both concepts, but neither he nor the meeting would be ignorant of the fact that Chalmers had written in favour of the first contention and Cunningham spoken positively of the second.

Burns spoke of his shock at the extent of what he called 'prejudice against colour', especially in the North and he was afraid that the cause of abolition in the States was far less advanced than the Society's report indicated. In moving the adoption of the Annual Report, Burns said he believed that if a Free Church delegation went now to America they would 'assume a much higher position with regard to the matter' (slavery). Nevertheless he did not think that they would give back the money. They didn't know to whom to give it back.

Rev. C.J. Kennedy of Paisley expressed his love and respect for Burns. However, he felt that, loving America as he did and hating slavery, the most moral choice would be for the Free Church to 'cast back every farthing of money that could be conceived to be tainted with slavery'. At this point the Chairman attempted to rule Mr Kennedy out of order, but the veteran abolitionist Dr John Ritchie of Potterrow United Secession Church, Edinburgh, argued that since Dr Burns had 'with all warrentable lattitude' taken an exception to the Report, Mr Kennedy was entitled to object to this. A speaker from America was happy to acknowledge the exceptions of churches who were against slavery, but had to tell the meeting that in his experience these same churches in the slave states 'submitted to slavery' and daren't speak against it. He was disappointed that the Free Church had not returned the money, for its acceptance had helped to take away the authority of the abolitionists in Scotland.

The Society in the end tried to hold the line for the moment, probably out of respect for the dilemma in which Robert Burns found himself. They were helped in this by an American visitor, Professor Wright, who pled with them not to seek the overthrow of the American Constitution, but to fight slavery through its avowed aim 'to establish justice'. This contrasted with the Professor's namesake Henry C. Wright, who had the previous year persuaded the Society to support the Garrisonian position, and would take them back to that before the year was out. Although the Society's Annual Meeting had, as the Free Church were attempting to do, put unity above radical action, the cracks very quickly appeared. The urgent need of being seen to take a stronger stand would soon be apparent.[3]

At a Public Meeting of Members and Friends of the Society in November 1844, Dr John Ritchie moved a resolution which started by recognising the concerns expressed by the Society over American slavery, but also the difficulty of knowing how to influence it in the right direction. With that in mind the Society was reminded that it had lately remonstrated with the Free Church 'in a friendly manner', and in support of American abolitionists, on the 'impropriety and impolicy of knowingly accepting contributions from acknowledged slaveholders, to provide the extension of the Gospel in Scotland'.

The resolution continued to express sadness at the 'indifference' with which the Free Church appeared to view the damaging effects of enabling the American church to proclaim that a Christian church in Scotland was favourable to slavery. Whilst wishing to 'cherish the outmost good feeling towards the Free Church', the Society wished to renew its protest at the reception of slave-holders money.

Henry C. Wright then moved that the Society, having learnt of the deliverances of the Candlish Commission of the Free Church, expressed 'deepest regret' that these were approved, emphasising that this would do 'obvious injury to the great cause of the abolition of slavery in the United States' and rightly or wrongly would be used in defence of slavery. The resolution continued by expressing concern that ministers from churches in America who sought to justify, rather than condemn slavery, could find their way into Free Church pulpits in Scotland. There was a proposed renewal of the protest 'against the reception by the Free Church or any other Evangelical Church of the contributions of slave-holders' and the mover, Dr John Ritchie, asked them to 'earnestly implore the Free Church, in a spirit of candour and faithfulness, to return to the donors their bloodstained offerings'.

The Society accepted this, and agreed to memorialise the Free Church and ministers of other denominations to raise a united voice in their attitude to the American churches, to refuse fellowship with slave-holding churches or pro-slavery ministers, and to deny them access to their pulpits. Dr Michael Willis read out the memorial and moved that the Committee, on which he sat, be instructed to give it maximum publicity.[4]

Sparks fly and die at the Free Presbytery of Edinburgh

On 12 March 1845, the Free Church Presbytery of Edinburgh met in a hall in the city's George Street. Dr John Duncan of New College proposed:

> That it be humbly overtured by this Presbytery to the General
> Assembly to give a clear and decided utterance on the subject
> of slavery; that it address an affectionate but faithful and
> uncompromising remonstrance to those churches stained with
> it, especially those who have expressed their sympathy with
> us; and that it order that any monies which may have been
> received from churches in which slave-owners are admissible
> to membership be kept separate and held unemployed until
> such time as these churches shall have professed repentance
> and proved it by reformation.

Short of returning the money and breaking fellowship, this proposed
deliverance went as far as any proposal in meeting the demands
of the abolitionists. Duncan himself was a formidable figure in
any company. A distinguished Professor of Old Testament and
Semitic Languages at the new Free Church College, he was known
affectionately as 'Rabbi' and in the *Annals of the Free Church* he was
described with his long beard and flowing robes as 'half ancient
mariner and half wandering Jew'.

Duncan argued that although slavery was not forbidden in
scripture, it violated the whole spirit of Christianity. In detailing the
horrors of its application in America he was highly critical of the
way that the American churches accommodated themselves to the
evil. 'It was monstrous' he said 'that Christians should regard their
fellow creatures subjected to this bondage as no better than beasts
or things, or, as they were termed, 'chattels personal'. The report in
the *Edinburgh Advertiser* stated that 'the learned Doctor eloquently
descanted on the inhumanities practised in this respect . . . which
would horrify even the incredulous.'.

Dr. Duncan declared himself incredulous that there 'ministers
who would sit down and eat the Lord's Supper with such unmakers
of men –– of traders in human blood.'. He knew that there were good
and pious men in the American churches but that simply for him
compounded the matter. They were 'lending the weight of their
character to the sanction of the enormity'.

He continued by arguing that the Free Church must take an
uncompromising stand on the issue. He feared that the Commission
of Assembly dealt 'too tenderly' with it and that its 'trumpet blew an
uncertain sound'. This attitude to a gross evil was, for him, a great
mistake. In a couthy way he referred to the mild expressions of the
Free Church's criticism of American slavery as 'soft sawder'[5] and
knowing that the American church money was 'in the coffers of the
Free Church', the Americans, for him 'might be apt to suppose that

they had thereby secured the silence of the Free Church upon their national sin'. 'Was it thus', asked Duncan, 'that every Free Church erection was to have a slave stone it?' An action that in his view would mean that they all had blood on their hands. In sharp contrast to Thomas Chalmers's reluctance to be too hard on the American churches, Duncan argued that to exert firmness at this stage would be a kindness to them.

Dr Henry Grey enthusiastically seconded the motion, going even further when he asked tellingly – 'Have we separated ourselves from our Moderate brethren [those remaining in the Church of Scotland] to form an alliance with man-stealers?' He instanced even more of the horrors of slavery, telling the Presbytery that women were flogged for refusing prostitution and men for wishing to hear the gospel. 'The slavery that is now in operation in the Southern states', he concluded, was not only irreconcilable with Christian principles but incompatible with Christian practice. 'We have borne our testimony against error in doctrine', said Grey, 'Let us not be less earnest in witnessing against error in practice. Either Christianity must expel slavery root and branch, or it will surely extirpate Christianity'.

There seemed now to be a groundswell in favour of strong action, not only from the Glasgow emancipationists, but from a leading Presbytery in the Free Church. But no sooner had the deliverance been moved and seconded than it started its slippery slope towards oblivion. The formidable forces of Drs Cunningham and Candlish then proceeded to destroy it. Cunningham appeared to embrace this task with more enthusiasm than his colleague. When he was a student he was reputed to be firmly attached to the Moderate party of the Church and his conservatism in church affairs was also reflected in his support for the Tory party. He was said to have only read *John Bull,* the patriotic London newspaper that embraced the cause of slavery and received contributions from the West Indian party in Parliament. Several years later he became an enthusiast for evangelical religion and was very much influenced by Dr Andrew Thomson.[6] Yet Thomson's uncompromising zeal for the abolition of slavery never caused Cunningham to make that same transition.

Cunningham began by complaining about the 'annoyance and inconvenience' caused to him by such discussions and saying that he felt it necessary to correct such erroneous statements. With scant respect for his colleagues, he accused Duncan of ignoring scripture and logic at the same time. Repeating once again his protestation that he hated the evils of slavery as strongly as anyone, Cunningham argued that the picture presented of the reality of slavery was faulty, and that the abolitionists, of whom he was highly critical, had 'ferociously assailed the churches' in the belief that 'whatever excellences men possessed, slavery deprived them of them all'.

He then took up two familiar positions to justify continuing fellowship with slave-holding churches. He was convinced that slave-owning had been no barrier to Christian fellowship in the church of the apostles, and he was equally convinced that American slave-owners, often the inheritors of slaves, had the burden thrust upon them. Even if that was not the case, in some states they could not obtain domestic servants unless they purchased slaves. Abolitionists, he insisted, made 'vague and unfounded charges', labelling churches that wouldn't expel slave-owners as 'man-stealers, thieves and robbers' and he ended with a total rejection of the notion that the church was called to break fellowship with slave-owners.

Candlish deplored any impression that the Free Church's horror of slavery was weaker than it was, or their satisfaction with the American churches stronger than the reality, and deprecated 'the raising of questions, the tendency of which was to keep asunder the Churches in that land'. Both he and Cunningham reminded the Presbytery that the abolitionists a decade ago never thought of breaking fellowship with missionaries in the West Indies who were forced to make many compromises and were to maintain silence on slavery. Turning to Duncan's arguments, he asked whether they were to be obliged to search the ancestry or genealogy of every penny that came into their exchequer. He ridiculed the idea of keeping the money in suspense and moved that the Overture be not transmitted to the General Assembly and that the matter be left in the hands of the forthcoming Assembly.

Grey attempted to rescue things by showing the deep involvement in slavery of even the leaders of many American churches, many of whom owned and bought and sold slaves, and by pointing out that the churches had now retracted or modified the strong opposition to slavery taken in the late eighteenth-century. But Duncan, after making a few observations in reply to Candlish, surprisingly agreed to withdraw the part of his motion that related to the use of the money. He was then persuaded to withdraw the entire motion and victory was conceded to the establishment of the Free Church in the persons of Drs Cunningham and Candlish. Such an easy caving in by Grey and Duncan did not augur well for the abolitionist cause in May. [7]

In the meantime the response to the Presbytery's position from the Glasgow Emancipation Society was swift. Three days afterwards the Committee approved a letter to the elders and members of American churches calling them to withdraw communion from slave-holders, and instructed the Secretaries to send copies to all ministers of the Free Church, requesting that it be read to and signed by, congregations and Kirk Sessions and then returned to the Society. It further approved a letter from H.C. Wright to Cunningham which was expanded and published later on in 1845 under the title, *American Slavery proved to be theft and robbery which no circumstances can justify or palliate.*

Reacting to Cunningham's distaste for denouncing slave-owners as man-stealers, Wright quoted Exodus 22.1, 'Whoever stealeth a man and selleth him shall be put to death' and cited John Wesley the founder of Methodism, who wrote in 1777 that 'man-buyers were as guilty as man-stealers' and 'thy hands, thy bed, thy furniture (Wright added 'thy churches') are stained with blood'. But, argued Wright, Cunningham declared that these same authors, abettors, and promoters of the diabolical slave-trade in America, may be respectable, useful, honoured orthodox Christians. 'Dr. Cunningham may say', continued Wright, 'it is shere madness to be denouncing every man who buys and holds a slave as a man-stealer', but William Pitt, Charles James Fox and John Wesley amongst others had, he said, done just that.

Wright claimed that Cunningham had refused to meet with abolitionists, but enjoyed the luxury and hospitality of the slave-owners without seeing plantation conditions. In fact Cunningham hardly touched the South in his travels, and apart from the time in Washington, he was unlikely to have encountered slave-owners at all. But it made for good polemic, as did Wright's concluding paragraph:

> If you justify holding and using men as beasts and things
> *under all circumstances* and join hands in Christian fellowship
> with those in America who make merchandise of the image
> of God – you must be entered upon the record of time and
> eternity as promotors and abettors of man-stealing, and of all
> the crimes and pollutions of American slavery.[8]

Dialogue between the Free Church leadership and the abolitionists was never a remote possibility, and least of all likely between Cunningham and Wright. Wright, whilst a powerful speaker and writer, was, as we shall see, too much of a loose cannon in the abolitionist camp. Cunningham, however, was resolute in his conservatism, and commanded enough power to keep the lid on the volcano of anti-slavery through the next Assembly and for the next nine months. Henry Grey had an interesting letter in *The Witness* later in the month when he admitted that his Presbytery speech showed 'over anxious jealousy in a good cause' and he had been glad to hear from Cunningham 'a more explicit avowal than we had before of the sinfulness of slavery'. He ended by writing:

> There are others with whom anti-slavery measures can be carried out but I own the disappointment would be very grievous to me and the ardour of my hope and confidence if the General Assembly could come to an infirm and compromising conclusion on this important question.[9]

The disappointment was all too soon to become real, but Henry Grey was not prepared to risk disunity in the church.

The 1845 General Assembly– discussion stifled for the sake of 'unity'

When the General Assembly met in late May 1845 the Free Church leaders could not have trodden more lightly on the issue of slavery and invited the Assembly to follow them. Robert Candlish on Monday 2 June, towards the end of the Assembly's business, was invited to give the report of his committee. The interim report given to and accepted by the Commission of Assembly could, he thought, have meant that the Committee regarded themselves discharged from any further action. Nonetheless, he felt that some further explanation was needed on some points in it, which he believed had been misunderstood.

Candlish wanted to reiterate the universal conviction in the Free Church that slavery was a 'heinous sin' and 'an accursed system', which carried with it 'national guilt' and the judgement of a righteous God. It was, he claimed, the duty of Christians 'to exert themselves to the utmost' to ensure its ending. Strong words, but he then went on to choose his words more carefully when he said the only divergent views within the Free Church were over the duties of the churches in America, 'who are called to deal partially with the evils of slavery, when it forms part of the social system in the community in which they are placed'. Already the edge of condemnation was blunted by Candlish's inference that some weight must be given to the fabric of Southern society into which slavery was inextricably woven.

'Even as to this matter', he continued, 'the difference is more apparent than real'. All are agreed, he said, that despite what the civil law allows, for a Christian person to treat a slave as a chattel is 'a sin of the deepest die' and would warrant such a person being excluded from the Christian communion. He could not agree that slave-holding as such was a cause for excommunication, but there was an obligation for all to seek manumission of their slaves. In the event of that being impossible, inhuman treatment, the denial of 'domestic relations', or of religious education, would be sufficient warrant for being banned from Christian fellowship.

Many in the Assembly must have felt that the Candlish Committee had travelled far along the road towards taking a strong stand to distance Christianity and slavery. But some of the more perceptive would have realised, and shortly American abolitionists were to make very clear, the impossible nature of the distinctions which Robert Candlish tried to make. As Harriet Beecher Stowe was to show several years later in *Uncle Tom's Cabin,* the use of the whip and the break up of families, the status of the slave as a chattel and the legal ban on teaching slaves to read, were not the aberrations of cruel masters (though all of them were embraced by these), but had been, and remained, an integral part of the whole system of American slavery.

Candlish then turned to the issue of church-to-church relations. He freely admitted to what he called 'considerable supineness' in the American churches regarding slavery and a reluctance to engage with it, adopting 'an apologetic tone in the treatment of it'.

However, he felt that the real question was whether the Free Church, brought into fellowship by God's providence with the American churches, was bound 'to refuse the tokens of their attachment which their people have given, and to renounce and repudiate all further friendly conversation with them'. Unsurprisingly his conclusion was that this was not the right course, and the one that he recommended to the Assembly was to continue in friendly conversation, 'faithfully exhorting and admonishing them to a full discharge of their duty'. If, as he believed, the Assembly should stop short of breaking off relationships with that church, he affirmed that there was no limit to the efforts that should be made by the Free Church to remonstrate with those who, he said, 'are placed in such difficult circumstances, in order that they may be found faithful'.

The skilled mixture of the moral and the pastoral approach taken by Candlish and his Committee virtually ensured that there would be no strong challenge to the American churches. A motion was proposed by Candlish to the effect that the Assembly approve the report, re-appoint the Committee, keep a watching brief on the situation, and report to the 1846 Assembly.

The seconder for the motion was John Duncan. Gone was the fiery rhetoric which had characterised his long speech on slavery at the Presbytery several months previously. He simply said that there might

CONTEMPORARY PROFESSORS OF NEW COLLEGE, EDINBURGH
DR. BANNERMAN   DR. SMEATON
DR. JAMES BUCHANAN   PRINCIPAL CUNNINGHAM   DR. DUNCAN

The Staff of New College, Edinburgh

be 'incidental phrases and views which did not come up entirely to his views of the question', but when he looked at the document as a whole he thought it was 'the best and most efficient course that the Court [Assembly] could employ'. Almost as a last flicker of his former radical stance, Duncan said that 'he continued to feel the most anxious concern' and then declared his 'perfect confidence in any proceeding of the Committee'. Henry Grey expressed his pleasure at the harmony arrived at. He too raised a muted reservation in that the 'expressions' on slavery appeared to be 'a little too general', but agreed that it was a 'step in the right direction'. He hoped that it would encourage individuals in the Church in America to 'do their duty on this question'.

In a tone that appeared to be irritated by the continuing discussion, Cunningham said that he hoped that there would be no further discussion on the subject. But since Messrs Duncan and Grey had ventured to add some remarks, he would do so also. He entirely concurred with the report and believed that few ministers in the American churches would dissent from it. He himself, however, doubted that 'considering the many features of this our country, there lay any direct and immediate responsibility on that Church, in the matter of American slavery, as to lay them under any duty to bring forward their views in regard to it at all'. It didn't seem to be clear whether 'that Church' referred to the Free Church or the American Presbyterian Church. At any rate, it was a dampening note and led to Dr John Smyth of St. George's Free Church in Glasgow to commend such unity and moderation, but to say also that he felt strongly that they should, as the Free Church, 'raise this solemn protest against 'slavery in general and American slavery in particular'.[10] The lid could not be kept on the volcano indefinitely.

Letters to and from America

Two very different communications between Scotland and America ensured that there would be an eruption in the near future. A response to the Candlish Committee's letter of autumn 1844 was sent to the Free Church on 27 May 1845, after the Presbyterian Church in America had met in their Assembly. Because of the overlap in the dates of the two Assemblies, the letter would not go before the Free Church as a body until May 1846. By that time the American Anti-Slavery Society, had sent three emissaries to Scotland, encouraged and hosted by the Glasgow Emancipation Society.

The response of the American Presbyterian Church in May 1845 contained a friendly letter and a copy of their own response to Memorials (petitions) on slavery which came from several Northern churches. The letter began with admiration for the courageous and faithful path taken by the Free Church, and appreciation for the visit of the delegation. It continued to assure their brothers in Scotland that the divisions in their church were being turned into unity, and that they appreciated 'the candour' with which the Free Church addressed the subject of slavery and their sharing of responsibility for its evils. It then somewhat ominously celebrated the freedom of the Free Church from any state control and linked it with the expectation that the American churches and the American state did not interfere with each other, not least over the issue of slavery. The concern for unity in the church was emphasised, alongside the reminder that slavery existed in the early church and that the early disciples did not see anything wrong with it.

The letter then went on to describe three categories of Memorials received by the Presbyterian Church. The first group called for amelioration of slave conditions, the second encouraged defiance of laws forbidding literacy amongst slaves, and the third called for the disciplining of any members who are slave-owners. In response to this, the letter assured the Free Church that the Presbyterian Church in America was unable to denounce slavery as a sin, since, it argued, Christ's teaching did not indicate this, and therefore slave-owners could not be excluded from the church. Having said that, they wanted to emphasise that they could not regard slaves as property nor sanction the separation of families or trafficking of slaves for 'filthy lucre' or 'the convenience of the master'.

The presence of George Lewis and William Chalmers at the American Presbyterian Assembly in 1844 and the concerns of the Free Church of Scotland expressed by the Candlish Committee's interim report, at least forced the Americans to respond to the Memorials. Two resolutions were passed by 168 votes to 13 and reported to the Free Church. They very clearly indicated that there were higher ecclesiastical and political priorities which could not be risked by challenging human bondage. They stated:

> 1st That the General Assembly of the Presbyterian church in the United States was originally organised, and has continued the bond of union in the church upon the conceded principle that the existence of domestic slavery, under the circumstance in which it is found in the southern portion of the country, is no bar to Christian communion.
>
> 2nd That the petitions that ask the Assembly to make the holding of slaves in itself a matter of discipline, do virtually require this judiciary to dissolve itself, and abandon the organisation under which, by the divine blessing, it has so long prospered. The tendency is evidently to separate the northern from the southern portion of the church; a result which every good citizen must deplore as tending to the dissolution of the union of our beloved country, and which every enlightened Christian will oppose, as bringing a ruinous and unnecessary schism between brethren who maintain a common faith.[11]

It would not be hard to find many thousands of black enlightened Christians who would see the continuation of domestic slavery a far more ruinous challenge to faith than a split in the church. But of course no one would have considered consulting them. For the sake of placating the Southern churches that had long held them to ransom, the Presbyterian Church in America had resolutely set their face against any action on slavery. Over the next decades, the fragmentation of the Presbyterian Church took place, partly in the 1850s, and culminating in the final break in 1861 at the start of the Civil War. It took one-hundred-and-twenty years to heal. In the meantime it was an American slave, hot foot from Boston, who was to lift the lid on the volcano in Scotland.

purpose they say in the next place we are in the pay of the establishment sent for and hired by them. Thus they give us a good reputation by classing us with persons against whose moral characters, they dare not utter a single word. The agitation goes nobly on - all this region is in a ferment. The very boys in the streets are singing out _Send back that money_. I am informed this morning by the Dundee courier that the St. Peters Session have unanimously recommended the sending back the money. I meet many free church people, who are anxious to have the money sent back. I am certain that the people are right on this point & if the money is not sent back it will be the fault of their leaders. We shall continue with unabated zeal to sound the alarm - the people

Letter from Frederick Douglass to Richard Webb

Chapter 5
'Douglass has blawn sic a flame'

Can we haud be it? Naw. Douglass has blawn sic a flame
That we winna hae peace till that siller's sent hame
Popular contemporary parody in verse

Self-liberated and strong

On 15 January 1846, under a week after arriving in Scotland, Frederick Douglass made his first speech in Scotland. The meeting in Glasgow was organised by his sponsors, the Glasgow Emancipation Society. Although he was not the first African American to address a public meeting in Scotland, as a self-liberated slave he commanded considerable attention from audiences sympathetic to the cause. In a early letter home he wrote to the Francis Jackson, President of the Massachusetts Anti-Slavery Society, 'it is quite an advantage to be a nigger here. I find I am hardly black enough for British taste, but by keeping my hair as woolly as possible I make out to pass for at least half a negro at any rate'.[1]

Douglass was born on a plantation in Maryland around 1817. His mother Harriet was a slave and his father was almost certainly the plantation owner, hence his mixed race appearance. At the age of twelve he was sold to another master, suffering the familiar tearing apart of the family, normal in chattel slavery. In 1838, by now a skilled worker, he escaped from the brutal treatment of overseers and made contact with the strong circle of abolitionists in the Boston area. Although earning a living as a ship's caulker in New Bedford, his skills of oratory were recognised by the Massachusetts abolitionists who engaged him as a lecturer. By this time he had a wife and four children, but the threat of recapture was always present, and the Anti-Slavery Society sent him in August 1845 on a two year speaking tour of Ireland, Scotland and England. From Ireland where he had much success, he arrived in Scotland in January 1846. For most of the time he was accompanied by James Buffum, a Massachusetts carpenter, but Buffum was very much the supporting speaker.

Douglass was widely read and entirely self-taught in the years since he fled from slavery. He rejected the name 'Bailey', given him by his master, and having a somewhat romantic view of Scotland based on Sir Walter Scott, but veering towards 'Braveheart', he saw the Douglas's as the standard bearers of freedom and decided to adopt the name, albeit with a slight amendment. He wrote back to the States about 'the free hills of old Scotland where . . . scarcely a stream but has been poured into song, or a hill that is not associated with some fierce and bloody conflict between liberty and slavery'.[2]

Although well instructed in the Free Church controversy, Douglass did not immediately address it. In his first, and well publicised, speech he took time to acquaint his audience, from direct personal experience, with the reality of American slavery. To cries of 'shame' and applause from the audience, he detailed the dire punishments handed out to slaves who dared to read the Bible or teach the Lord's Prayer to their children. Douglass skilfully drew the distinction between chattel slavery and the so called slave conditions of workers in Britain, then turned to underscore the responsibility of the churches for maintaining the system. 'Would you', he asked his audience, 'belong to a church that held fellowship with slaveholders . . . with the man-stealing, cradle-robbing, woman-beating American slave-holder?' [3]

Douglass knew exactly how to measure his words. He was aware that, as in the West Indies, so in the Southern States, those who depended on the system were keen to sanitise it by promoting the slave-owners as benevolent, and the cruelties as rare aberrations. In his personal story he showed that the theft and sale of human beings, physical degradation and torture, and the breaking up of families were integral to the whole operation of slavery. From Glasgow he went to Dundee, hosted by sympathetic ministers, including the celebrated literary figure and local Secessionist minister, Rev. George Gilfillan. Gilfillan two years later gave a published lecture, *The debasing and demoralising influence of slavery on all and everything connected with it*. He was keen to show that no amount of kindness or any number of 'good' masters would mitigate the horrors of slavery, but equally to demonstrate that slavery could not break the human spirit of the slaves. 'You have seen in Frederick Douglass', he stated, 'a man whom slavery has not nipped, but developed'. Gilfillan was a kindred spirit with Douglass. It was in Dundee that the 'Send Back the Money' campaign was set alight.

In the first of four public meetings in the city at the end of January 1846, Douglass broached the Free Church question. He was at pains to say that he offered no criticism of the Free Church in its break with the Church of Scotland, and he would not comment on the rights or

Frederick Douglass

wrongs of the Disruption. He recognised that some might wish to present the American abolitionists (he and Buffen had been joined by Henry C. Wright) as the paid servants of other churches wishing to destroy the Free Church. His business however was solely on slavery, and he wished to quote from the Old Testament. 'I should find it impossible', he said, 'to draw a more graphic picture of the state of the churches in the United States than is drawn from the holy prophet Isaiah', when he tells Israel 'your hands are full of blood'.

Send Back the Money

From the wide polemical sweep Douglass then turned to the Free Church's arguments to justify continued fellowship with the American churches. He was well briefed that George Lewis, by no means the least critical of slavery in the United States, but part of the Free Church delegation, was a prominent minister in the city. At first he simply asked where Lewis had been in the South, and what he had been allowed to see, even challenging him to a debate on the subject, one that Lewis rejected. But at a meeting on 10 March at George Gilfillan's Chapel, he turned up the heat by making a series of charges against the Free Church – 'accepting money from well known thieves to build her churches and pay her ministers', 'following the bidding of slaveholders and their guilty abettors, whilst they turn a deaf ear to the bleeding and whip-scored slave', and 'having adopted the name of "Free Church", while they are doing the work of a slave church'. Douglass then turned to imagine the scene if 'brother Lewis' had called on his old master to ask for a subscription. Mr Auld would be moved by the plight of the Free

Church in its struggle for Gospel freedom in Scotland, and would
have sold one of his young slaves, such as Douglass, to release funds
for his own donation. 'Brother Lewis prays' continued Douglass
'and reads "blessed are those who give to the poor", as Auld ties the
slave to his carriage and takes him off for auction.

Just as a mixture of applause and ironic laughter was heard from
his audience, Douglass, with great debating skill, moved to his
peroration, and for the first time the repeated refrain of 'Send back
the Money' became a catch phrase, cheered at every mention. 'When
the Free Church says did not Abraham hold slaves?' thundered
Douglass:

> The reply should be, Send back that money! When they ask
> did not Paul send back Onesimus? I answer, Send you back
> that money! That is the only answer Which should be given to
> their sophisticated arguments, and it is one that they cannot
> get over. In order to justify their conduct they endeavour
> to forget that they are a church and speak as if they were a
> manufacturing corporation. They forget that a church is not
> for making money, but for spreading the Gospel. We are
> guilty, say they, but these merchants are guilty and some other
> parties are guilty also. I say, send back that money. There is
> music in the sound. There is poetry in it.

Although Douglass must have been aware of the veneration in
which Thomas Chalmers was held, the Free Church leader's attempt
to justify accepting the money and remaining in fellowship with
the American church, led to some of the abolitionist orator's most
passionate broadsides. The argument made by Chalmers that
American slave-owners could not just release their slaves, and had
to live within the framework of the law, was greeted with scorn by
Douglass. 'If the law were to say that we were to worship Vishnu or
any heathen deity', he asked, 'would that be right because it was the
law?' And he went on to recall the familiar Old Testament heroes
Shadrach, Meshach and Abednego who faced death by fire, rather
than submit to the Babylonian decree to stop worshipping God.
'Had these doctors (Chalmers, Cunningham and Candlish) lived
in these days they would have bowed down to the golden image',
said Douglas to the Dundee audience. 'What I would advise, says
Dr Chalmers, is to submit to the powers that be . . . worship only in
form but not in heart; you may be lifting up your hearts to the Lord,
and thus save your lives and your principles also'. The audience
responded with 'great cheering and laughter'.[4]

This charge of trimming for convenience was one which Douglass repeated as he moved further up the east coast to Arbroath. Nothing riled him more than Chalmers's assertion that 'a distinction must be made between the character of a system (slavery) and the character of a person whom circumstances have implicated therein'. For Douglas this gave licence to absolve murderers, adulterers, and thieves from the consequences of their actions. 'Oh the artful Dodger!' he described Chalmers, and continued:

> What an excellent outlet for sinners! Let slave-owners rejoice! Let a fiendish glee run round and round through hell! Dr. Chalmers, the eloquent Scotch divine, has, by long study and deep research, found that . . . while slavery be a heinous sin, the slave-owner may be a good Christian, the representative of the blessed Saviour on earth, an heir of heaven and eternal glory, for such is what is implied by Christian fellowship.[5]

Such direct attacks of course inevitably led to enmity towards Douglass. A Dundee newspaper, *The Northern Warder*, accused him of being in the pay of the Church of Scotland and many churches in Arbroath were closed to him. In Paisley, in March, he returned to the theme of George Lewis collecting money from those, like his former master, who gave generously from the proceeds of slave sales, and the 'send back the money' phrase was a familiar one at the close of his speeches. But he returned to the broad theme of educating his audience in the true horrors of American slavery. In Ayr at the end of March, Douglass expressed pleasure in meeting 'those who in sympathising affection, assemble to consider the wrongs of their race'. 'I am here tonight', he continued:

> To let you know the wrongs, the miseries, and the stripes of three millions of human beings for whom the Saviour died; and though time would fail me to give all the details of the horrid system by which they are held, I yet hope to place before you sufficient facts to enlist your sympathies in their behalf.

Douglass was careful to pay tribute to those in Britain who had been pioneers in the campaign to abolish the slave trade and West Indian slavery. At a soiree (evening social gathering) in honour of himself and James Buffum in Paisley, he commended the pioneering work of Granville Sharp and the Quaker stirrings against the slave-trade in the late eighteenth-century. At the mention of William Wilberforce and Thomas Clarkson there was huge cheering, although the absence of prominent Scottish abolitionists such as William Dickson, James Stephen and Zachary Macaulay, indicated a gap in his knowledge of that time. Inspired by that heritage he called for what he termed 'an

International Moral Force' to destroy slavery, and he ended another address to 1200 citizens of Paisley in April 1846 with this rallying cry:

> Dr Chalmers has said that it would be most unjustifiable to deny the slaveholder Christian fellowship. Scotland and the slaveholder at one! Shall it be so? [Shouts of No! No!] The people are with us in Arbroath, Dundee, Aberdeen, Montrose, Greenock, Glasgow – and they will be with us in Edinburgh [loud applause] We wish to have Scotland, England, Ireland, Canada, Mexico, even the Red Indians with us and against slavery. We want to have the whole country surrounded with an anti-slavery wall, with the words legibly inscribed thereon, Send Back the Money, Send Back the Money [Long continued cheering].[6]

Temperance and Opposition

Douglass skilfully tapped another popular cause to make the link with slavery. Drink and its social effects had long been a public concern in Scotland and the Temperance movement (effectively the call for abstinence) by this time attracted great support, especially amongst the middle classes who could drink quietly at home. Buffum and Douglass attended a large gathering in Glasgow's City Hall in February 1846, attended by temperance enthusiasts from Scotland and the north of England. Buffum spoke on 'the rise, progress, and results of the temperance movement in America', and after several hours of what the *Glasgow Examiner* termed 'unremitting oratory', Douglass rose to his feet. 'Slavery', he said, 'is a poor school for rearing moralists or reformers of any kind', but he wished to link it with drink in a very practical application. He explained how in Maryland, where he was brought up, it was common for masters to give slaves drink on a Saturday night 'to keep them during the Sabbath in a state of stupidity'. Drink was for Douglass a tool to dull the senses and avoid the risk of the slave, in his leisure time, thinking of freedom. To cheers from the crowd he thundered 'This intemperance enslaves – this intemperance paralyses – this intemperance binds with bonds stronger than iron, and makes man the willing subject of its brute control'.

Most of those who were hostile to Douglass, either voted with their feet or refused to have him in their churches. There was occasional dissent at meetings, such as some hissing in Dundee when he criticised George Lewis. One who voiced his opposition and defended the Free Church in a pamphlet, was Rev. John Macnaughton of Paisley.[7] In a speech on 21 April 1846 Macnaughton termed Douglass an 'ignorant runaway slave, who had picked up a few sentences which he was pleased to retail up and down the country', and expressed his surprise that Paisley's citizens paid money to hear him speak. Four days later Douglass responded. A number of churches, no doubt due to Macnaughton's intervention, were barred to him on the day he was due to speak. Paisley abolitionists, keen to see public discussion of the issue, took up Douglass's challenge to debate with Macnaughton and distributed handbills, but the latter never appeared.

Douglass repeated the accusation made that he was 'a poor, miserable, ignorant, fugitive slave'. He did not wish to comment on the position of 'that gentleman' nor to 'trace him to any extraordinary ancestors'. He then went on to analyse what he called 'a degree of audacity, which I did not expect to witness on the part of any Free Church clergyman'. 'The man', he said, 'who enjoys his share of the three thousand pounds taken from the slaveholder, and robbed from the slave, stands up to denounce me as being ignorant. Shame on him'. In an emotional piece of oratory which clearly showed his personal hurt, Douglass continued:

> I should like to see the inside of his breast; there cannot be a heart of flesh there. There must be a stone or a gizzard there. Let him launch out that gold and I shall undertake to educate a number of slaves, who will in a few years be able to stand by the side of Mr. Macnaughton. . . . Macnaughton has linked himself with the slaveholder, and he cannot therefore have any sympathy with a slave. The interest of the one is antagonistic to the other. The slave runs, and the slave-owner sets his dogs on him to catch him and bring him back . . . When a slave comes here to plead their cause, Macnaughton calls him a poor miserable fugitive slave. Macnaughton won't get rid of us by any such statements.[8]

Later that year, Douglass returned to Scotland after several months down south. Douglass claimed that the man he now called 'brother Macnaughton', had insulted Henry C. Wright too. But so much had Macnaughton's criticism of him as 'an ignorant fugitive' got under his skin, that Douglass returned to it when he was in Paisley in late September 1846. 'I have made these remarks', he said, 'because he [Macnaughton] has made very free with me elsewhere . . . at the time he was pocketing the money wrung from the souls of my own brethren in slavery. He denounces me for my ignorance. I say such a man is not worthy to be called a Christian minister'.

These words were said from the platform of what was described 'The Great Anti-Slavery Meeting', held in Rev. Robert Cairns's Secession Church in Paisley 23 September 1846. Douglass was accompanied by the veteran American abolitionist and editor of *The Liberator* William Lloyd Garrison. Garrison, another invitee of the Glasgow Emancipation Society, who was very much on the radical wing of the movement, believed in resistance to any authority, and unlike Douglass, with whom he split eventually on the issue, saw no good in the American Constitution, nor any prospect of ridding the United States of slavery through normal democratic pressure. As a protégé of Garrison, Douglass was pleased to have his support at this stage, not least when he intervened to substitute the words 'slave-holder' and 'slave-holding' with those of 'robbery' and 'robber'.[9]

John Macnaughton of Paisley may have been the most vocal and direct opponent of Douglass, but he was not of course alone. Many other Free Church ministers, and some others, simply refused to have him speaking in their churches. On the other hand when Douglass thought that his visit to Aberdeen in March 1846 had simply met with a 'granite' reception, he learnt that there were many who wanted to hear him. On his departure, a petition was given to him from 'a large number of respected citizens', many of whom were from the Free Church. They told him that they had never authorised Lewis to 'form an alliance with slaveholders' or Chalmers 'to write a fraternal letter to a slaveholder in South Carolina'.

Although Douglass was never met with the racist taunt 'Send back the nigger', which he had experienced in Belfast, in an otherwise successful tour prior to his arrival in Scotland, some of his Scottish detractors came close to it. In May 1846 the conservative *Scottish Guardian*, referring to him as 'the black', sneered 'if American slavery were abolished tomorrow, their trade [the Abolitionists] would be gone. Mr. Douglass, we suppose, would instantly return to his more important duties as "a chimney sweeper."

A month earlier, on 11 April the *Scottish Guardian* published a letter by a correspondent who styled himself 'Veritas'. Douglass read it at a meeting in Paisley on 17 April. 'Veritas', who is thought to be William Gregor, a Church of Scotland minister, had been at a meeting addressed by Douglass and Buffum. He had listened to the horrors of slavery, but pled that there were two sides to the story. 'Veritas' had been in New York for eighteen months, and had 'seen the moral and religious character of the proprietors of the Southern States blackened by every means that self interest and the vilest hypocrisy could devise'. He was convinced that many slave-owners treated their slaves better than white workers in the north, and he accused 'Douglass and his constituents' of delusions. He advised 'the semi-savage Douglass', to be more 'tender-hearted in the applications of

his three toed thong to the back of Dr Chalmers and others', lest it
be turned on him and that 'Send Back the Money' might yet, after
all his pathos, be turned into 'Send Douglass back' to learn more
correctness in his statements, and more justice in his conclusions'.
Incredibly, 'Veritas' concluded with the statement that Douglass
'and his constituents' were 'inducing a morality incalculably more
immoral, savage, barbarous, bloody and brutal than that which he
affects so much to deplore', and that 'the Free Church delegation, in
appealing to the proprietors of the Southern States', acted, 'with an
impartiality, and upon principles of an enlightened philanthropy,
for which all ages shall bless them, especially the toil-worn millions'.
It was so extreme that Douglass declined to answer it.[10]

In full cry

Douglass told a London audience in May 1846, 'I am used to being
hissed in Scotland on the subject, for they do not like me to state the
thing in my own language'. It was one of the strengths of Douglass's
oratory that he used the starkest descriptive terminology. Frustrated
by the Free Church's incessant attempts to find fine distinctions
of guilt and absolution over slave-holding, whilst admitting that
in Robert Candlish's words slavery was 'a sin of the deepest die',
Douglass delighted in the free use of 'theft', 'banditry', 'man-
stealing', and 'murder'. In Arbroath he thundered:

> Good God! What a system! A system of blood and pollution;
> of infidelity and atheism; of wholesale plunder and murder.
> Truly did John Wesley denounce it as the sum of all villainies
> and the compendium of all crime. This, Christian friends, is
> but a faint picture of American slavery, and this is the system
> upheld and sustained by the entire church in the Southern
> States of the American Union. It is with such a church that
> the Free Church of Scotland is linked and interlinked in
> Christian fellowship. It is such a church that the Free Church
> of Scotland are trying to palm off to the world as a Christian
> Church. . . . The Free Church, in vindicating their fellowship
> of slaveholders, have acted on the damning heresy that a man
> may be a Christian whatever may be his practice, so his creed
> be right. So he pays tithes of mint, anise and cumin, he may be
> a Christian, though he totally reject judgement and mercy.[11] It
> is this heresy that now holds in chains three millions of men,
> women, and children in the United States.

Although not a theologian, Douglas did not hesitate to challenge the
Free Church on matters of heresy. He was, however, happier in the

cut and thrust of campaigning than arguing doctrinal niceties.

Storming the City Crags with 'Quakeresses'

Throughout Scotland's east coast youngsters were said to shout anti-slavery slogans or sing songs (Glasgow saw very little of such happenings despite the much more radical Emancipation Committee), Douglass reported this direct activism with glee. At a meeting in Paisley he stated that 'Send Back the Money' had been painted in red on a wall in Arbroath, representing slaves' blood, that all the efforts to remove it were to no avail. It was not a lone act. Many walls from the Tay to the Tweed saw similar slogans chalked or painted on them.

Rev. John Campbell told a meeting in London of how early one morning, 'this mighty man' Douglass climbed Arthur's Seat, the craggy hill visible from Edinburgh's city centre, and with the help of 'two fair Quakeresses', began to carve out with a spade 'Send Back The Money' on the grass. He was warned that this action was a felony, and he would be 'at the tender mercies of Baillie Gray' of the City Council. Campbell remarked that for a man who had faced the wrath of slave-owners, an Edinburgh Baillie would hardly make Douglass quake.[12] There is no other mention of these two 'Quakeresses' by him, but almost certainly they were Jane and Eliza Wigham.

Although there was a Quaker meeting-house in Glasgow as early as 1660, the track record of Quaker anti-slavery activity in the late eighteenth-century and early nineteenth-century in Scotland was as non-existent as it was pioneering in England and America. It could be reasonably argued that members of the Society of Friends were very few north of the border, but it was remarkable that in the decade between the abolition of slavery in the British Empire and the 'Send Back the Money' campaign, the Scottish Quakers had achieved such a significant and leading role amongst Scottish abolitionists. This was achieved by two families who were intertwined and originated from the north of England, the Smeals and the Wighams.

In his autobiography, Douglass listed William Smeal as one of the 'sterling anti-slavery men in Glasgow', who 'denounced the [Free Church] transaction as shocking and disgraceful to the religious sentiment of Scotland'.[13] Smeal was joint Secretary of the Glasgow Emancipation Society, and had invited Douglass, on their behalf, to the city where he acted as his host. He was a successful business man in the grocery trade. The collection of anti-slavery papers in Glasgow's Mitchell Library preserved by Smeal, is the surviving source of information on the city's abolition campaigns at this time.

Jane and Eliza Wigham were active in the Edinburgh Ladies Emancipation Society, which took a much stronger line on the Free Church's policy than its male counterpart. Jane was the sister of William Smeal, one of whose close friends was a fellow Quaker, Anthony Wigham, who had been one of the founding Secretaries of the Glasgow Society before moving to Aberdeen. Anthony's cousin, John Wigham, married William Smeal's sister Jane, whose stepdaughter was Eliza.

Of all the Quaker activists in Scotland, Eliza Wigham, who never married, was probably the most prominent, campaigning over a period that spanned three decades. In her introduction to her book on American anti-slavery, she outlined her philosophy of action. 'It is very important', she wrote, in the middle of the Civil War:

> To bear in mind the character of slavery, in order to estimate the urgency of the call which abolitionists felt bound to obey, 'to cry aloud and spare not'. It is also important to remember the intimate connection of slavery with the whole social, religious, and political organisation of America, in order rightly to appreciate the courage of those who began to assail it.[14]

It was a sentiment that would have the full approval of Frederick Douglass, and possibly reflected the conversations that Eliza had had with him twenty years previously. Although some earlier abolitionists in Britain such as William Wilberforce had been strongly opposed the visible presence of women in the cause, and in the 1840s no women spoke publically on anti-slavery platforms, Douglass clearly appreciated female support for such direct action.

The flame burns

In the first month of his Scottish tour Douglass wrote to Francis Jackson:

> Our efforts are directed to making them disgorge their ill-gotten gain – return it to the Slave-holders. Our rallying cry is "No union with Slave-holders and send back the blood-stained money." Under these rallying cries, old Scotland boils like a pot. It would indeed be a grand anti-slavery triumph if we could get her to send back the money. It would break upon the confounded slaveholder's sky – we shall continue to deal our? [writing obscured] upon them, crying out disgorge, disgorge, disgorge your horrid plunder, and to this cry thus far the great mass of people have cried "Amen, Amen".

The next month he was to write in similar vein to Richard Webb in

Dublin:

> The agitation goes nobly on – all this region is in ferment. The
> very boys in the street are singing out *'send back the money'*. I
> am informed this morning by the *Dundee Courier* that the St
> Peter's Session have unanimously recommended the sending
> back the money. I meet Free Church people who are anxious
> to have the money sent back. I am certain that the people are
> right on this point, and if the money is not sent back it will be
> the fault of their leaders. We shall continue with unabated zeal
> to sound the alarm – the people will be informed.[15]

There is no doubt that Douglas was a sensation in Scotland, and
that he drew large crowds. Buffum, Wright, and even the famed
Garrison, with their greater experience of the cause, were always
rated supporting speakers. George Gilfillan noted that Douglass was
'educated and endowed to destroy his cruel and unnatural mother'.

Two anonymous hearers paid tribute to him in different ways.
One who had heard him at a street corner meeting observed – 'the
spirit of the Lord is in the black as well as the white man – and the
inspiration of the almighty gave him understanding. How forcibly
he preached his people's wrong! Strong language indeed. Oh let us
be up to send back, not only the money, but the people'.

The other who would no doubt have greatly amused Douglass,
dwelt on his physical presence, and did so in broad Scots. He wrote:

> On Monday nicht our Jock got me to gang doun an' hear that
> chiel Douglass. I had came away wanting ma specks; but frae
> the luik I gat o' him, he seemed a burly fellow, ane I shouldna
> like to hae a tussle wi him either feeseecally or intellecktually.[16]

Douglass drew huge and overwhelmingly supportive crowds, and
there is no doubt that he succeeded in raising awareness in Scotland
of the reality of American Slavery.

At the same time his uncompromising stance inevitably left
no room for the leadership of the Free Church to manoeuvre, and
his strong and often satirical critique of figures such as Chalmers,
Cunningham, Candlish, Lewis and others prevented any possibility
of dialogue with the church leadership. In company with most great
orators, he exaggerated. Although the Free Church's refusal to deny
fellowship to the Southern churches was a psychological blow to
abolitionists in America, it was a comparatively small one. And to
claim that returning the money and denying acceptance of American
christians would shake the foundations of slavery, was a powerful
oratorical point, but had little practical basis. Nonetheless, Douglass
of all the anti-slavery protagonists of his time, was able to ignite

a flame in Scotland that burned for a time in many a household, church, and assembly.

Chapter 6
War, Drink, the Sabbath and the 1846 Assembly

There is no place in which a reformed drunkard is so irresistibly tempted to return to his wallowings in the filth of drunkenness, as to join a Church, to become an elder or a deacon, and to associate with ministers.
Henry C.Wright to William Lloyd Garrison, 28 March 1846

A loose cannon among the abolitionists

Henry C. Wright was perhaps best defined by what he no longer was. He was born in the closing years of the eighteenth-century and was a tradesman before entering theological college and proceeding to ordination as a Congregation minister. From ministering to a congregation in Massachusetts he became an agent of the American Anti-Slavery Society in 1835, which dismissed him after two years because of his extreme opinions that didn't fit their policy. At the same time he was asked to give up lecturing for the American Peace Society and before leaving to tour Europe from 1842–1847 he started the New England Non-Resistance Society. Wright was a pacifist, although he occasionally condoned violent responses to slavery. His knowledge, love, and use of the Bible remained throughout his life but he was a strong opponent of Sabbatarianism. Towards the end of his life he became a spiritualist. Two things were constant. He was a life-long believer in non-resistance – a kind of spiritual anarchist who prized individual conscience above all – and he opposed all forms of coercion. He was not an easy man to work with.

Douglass contrasted with Wright in various ways. The one read his audience well and was sensitive to where they were coming from. The other went headfirst into conflict and could be very clumsy. The one believed that slavery could be abolished by democratic means and through the constitution. The other wanted to get rid of the constitution and saw the American political system as incapable of redemption. The one was later close to President Abraham Lincoln and worked to recruit African Americans for the Union forces in the

Civil War. The other, although totally unsympathetic to the South, was fundamentally opposed to any war and would have no part in it. The one thing that they had in common was that both were to break with William Lloyd Garrison, Douglass much earlier than Wright.

Frederick Douglass made it clear that his mission in Scotland was solely to build up hostility to American slavery, primarily by exposing it in all its cruelty and horror, and to argue vehemently that any Christian church worthy of the name could not keep company with those who participated in the evil system. Realising the difficulty of persuading his audience to take an absolutist stand and of winning widespread support across broad frontiers of churchmanship, he was careful not to dilute the cause by flying other kites or introducing other causes. Even when he spoke at Temperance meetings or in Temperance halls, it was the foisting of drink on slaves to drug them and dull any thoughts of freedom that was his theme. Above all, he specifically refused to comment on the doctrine, practise, or attitude of the Free Church towards any other Churches, except in the matter of dealing with those who accepted slave-owners in their membership.

Henry C. Wright had no such inhibitions. His address to the Glasgow Emancipation Society in 1843 had been a full scale assault on the United States. In 1845 he published his attack on the position of Drs Cunningham and Candlish, and in 1846 his target was the American constitution as irredeemably flawed. It took the form of six letters, penned from his temporary home in Roseneath on the Clyde to his friend James Haughton of Dublin, written for publication.[1] Not only was Wright firmly aligned to one party in the increasingly divided abolition movement in America, but those of his Scottish audiences who might be nervous about a radical attack on all slave-owners in America, had their troubled spirits even more shaken.

In the Scotland at that time, the attack on the American Union was less shocking than Wright's other target – Sabbatarianism. In 1846 he produced another document which questioned the biblical evidence to justify the bleak and cheerless prohibitions associated with Sunday as 'The Lord's Day'. It was addressed in the form of a letter to the Committee of the moderate Edinburgh Emancipation Society, which had declined to work with him.

Wright's first plea was that whatever their differences on other subjects, Anti-Slavery should be a cause to unite them. 'I would not ask', he wrote, 'whether a man be a Jew, Mahometan, Heathen or Christian as a preliminary to cooperation in the abolition of slavery', a point of view that most in the twenty-first century would have warmed to, but less likely to win many votes in the mid nineteenth. Even then, if he had limited his case to the issue of anti-slavery uniting folk of diverse views, he might have had some influence. Instead he spent forty-five pages 'exposing' as he saw it, the error of insisting on keeping Sunday as a day apart. Wright claimed that the gospel and the early church practice, recorded in the book of Acts of breaking bread weekly, held no such warrant. To Calvinist Scotland he claimed that in book two of Calvin's *Institutes*, the Swiss Reformer had condemned 'those who far exceed the Jews in a gross, carnal, superstitious observance of the Sabbath, so that the reproofs we read of in the [Old Testament] book of Isaiah Ch.1.13 and Ch.58.13 apply as much to the present day, as those to whom the prophet addressed them'.

Not content with that, at the end of the document Wright condemned the repressive prohibition on children playing on a Sunday, and argued that the false teaching that one day was sacred, left a child without 'moral and religious restraints on his passions, his words and actions on other days which were operative on the first day'. He signed it 'Yours for truth'. [2]

It was small wonder that this brought both serious and ribald response. A curious document in May 1846 *The Yankee Looking Glass* by Dody Tomkins, mocked Wright as 'the friend of the slave and the enemy of the Free Church' and listed his allies as 'Socinians, Infidels, Mohemetans, Jews and Christians the more the merrier'. Often pamphlets appeared anonymously and one was addressed by 'a close observer', to the Managers in Edinburgh of Rose Street Secession Church and College Street Relief Church, whose minister, Rev. John French, had just been awarded a doctorate by Glasgow University. Both churches had invited Henry C. Wright to address them from the pulpit, and this was denounced by the writer. Whilst admitting that the Free Church had been wrong to receive the money, he questioned whether this was 'the Christian way to set her right'. 'If you wish to rebuke the Free Church', continued 'Observer', 'at least get one who believes in the Bible to do it. Do not hire a Sabbath breaker'. The anonymous pamphleteer made the telling point that Rose Street had itself received five hundred pounds and twelve acres of land from slave-holders. [3]

Anti-War was as equal an obsession for Henry C. Wright as Anti-Sabbatarianism. In 1846 he published a two-hundred-and-fifteen-page booklet entitled *Defensive War proved to be a denial of Christianity and the government of God with illustrative facts and anecdotes*. As the title suggests, much of it consisted of conversations with others, especially high ranking military officers, upon the ethics of war. It was accompanied by a whimsical piece sold by G.Gallie in Buchanan Street, Glasgow, entitled *A Book of interesting stories for children to show them how to live together without quarrelling*. This was priced at one shilling and sixpence, thus putting it out of range for most in Scotland. Wright seemed to lose touch with reality altogether since he published, also in 1846, at five shillings and sixpence, *Conversations on Non-Resistance and other subjects including a graphic report of the author's experience in the water cure of his treatment for the disease of the lungs under Priessnitz and the State of Society at Graefenberg.*

All this might suggest that Henry C. Wright was unbalanced. That would be too harsh a judgement. In many of his public appearances he made effective response to the weak, though scholarly, attempts by the three Free Church professors – Chalmers, Cunningham and Candlish – to justify the Free Church's refusal to cut ties with churches that included slave-owners in their membership. In his *Appeal to Members and Ministers of the Free Church*, he asked trenchant, if dramatic, questions about whether money would ever have been given if a stand against slavery had been taken by the delegates to America. He invited his readers to imagine the price of ransoming Dr Cunningham, had he been seized and sold. He asked the rhetorical question whether in the eyes of Christ every African was not of the same value as any of other races? [4]

In Wright's published letters from Rochane Cottage, Roseneath, he skilfully took the words of respected Free Church leaders to challenge their policy. He quoted Duncan's question at the 1845 Presbytery of Edinburgh about every church having 'a slave stone' and the Old Testament scholar's refusal to take communion with 'traders in human flesh'. Almost more tellingly, Wright cited Henry Grey of Edinburgh who, while Moderator of the 1844 General Assembly, had attempted to broker peace in the Assembly. Grey had nonetheless expressed himself forcefully on the side of the abolitionists when, at Presbytery, he had asked the question that Wright repeated in full:

Have we separated ourselves from our Moderate brethren to form alliance with man-stealers? Do we remove from us a brother that walketh disorderly – a drunkard, a fornicator, an adulterer, to unite ourselves with man-stealers, sellers of their own offspring, stained with the blood of innocents, leprous with sin? [5]

The Hawick Alcoholics

Henry C. Wright could be extremely skilful but his obsession with so many causes weakened the effectiveness of his abolition work. If it was only that, the cause might have been diluted, but not damaged. We have already seen the problems caused by his strong anti-sabbatarian views. The greatest difficulty, however, was caused by his intemperate and often ill informed personal accusations. After the 'Synod' (his word!) of Montrose argued in favour of keeping the money, Wright accused Rev. William Nixon, minister of the town's Free Church, of 'burying his child on a Sunday', an insensitive and callous remark. [6]

Wright's carelessness about what he wrote, and to whom, backfired badly in 1846. A letter sent to Garrison from Melrose on 28 March found its way to *The Witness*. 'I wish to call attention', he wrote:

To the fact that in Scotland and in England the most dangerous place in which a reformed drunkard could place himself in society is IN THE CHURCH. There is no place in which a reformed drunkard is so irresistibly tempted to return to his wallowings in the filth of drunkenness, as to join a Church, to become an elder or a deacon, and to associate with ministers. He would be more likely to become a drunkard in Dr Wardlaw's or Dr Chalmers' church and at their dinner-tables than in the lowest grog-shop in Glasgow or Edinburgh, for the simple reason that at the dinner and communion tables of Doctors Chalmers and Wardlaw, the tippling custom is adorned with the charms of social elegance and respectability, and sanctified by prayer![7]

Earlier that month copies of Garrison's *Liberator* had arrived in Hawick from Boston. The local newspaper *Border Watch* reproduced from the paper, parts of what it claimed was a letter from Robert Michie, 'a respectable currier in Hawick' to Henry C. Wright. Michie, who strongly supported the 'Send Back the Money Campaign', was quoted there as alleging that the Free Church minister in Hawick, Rev. John Aikman Wallace, allowed drunkards into the Free Church when previously he had excluded them from the Church of Scotland. Worse still, Michie reported that 'A.R.', a reformed drunkard in the town, now returned to the church, had been led astray 'by the tippling habits of his minister Mr. Wallace and the elders'. Michie claimed that 'A.R' tasted the fire-water' and was ruined. He had begged Michie to help him, claiming that Wallace and the elders had never remonstrated with him. Michie invited him to go to the parish church (Church of Scotland) to hear Rev. John Macrae, but he said 'degraded as he was, he would never sink as low as that'.

When this account reached Robert Michie, he immediately wrote to Rev. John Wallace regretting ever criticising the Free Church and emphatically denying the 'tippling' example. 'I never thought this', he claimed, and continued, 'the person who has so altered my letter and taken such liberties with my name, has wronged me grievously'. Michie demanded a return of his letter. Wright blamed the Boston printer, and said that the letter had now been burnt. Following an apology from Michie, Wallace pressed for the whole affair to be closed, but the Deacons Court of Hawick Free Church insisted that the whole proceedings be recorded in a pamphlet.[8] The incident assumed the nature of a farce, but it undoubtedly damaged the cause of the abolitionists.

The 1846 Assembly: A debate about no debate

The Free Church gathered in General Assembly at the end of May 1846. For the new Moderator, Rev. Robert Brown of Aberdeen, it was going to be a difficult week. On Saturday 20 May he informed the Assembly that memorials on American slavery had been received from the Glasgow Emancipation Society and the British and Foreign Anti-Slavery Society, and a remonstrance from the Edinburgh Ladies Emancipation Society. Although the Moderator was easily able on procedural grounds (they had not passed through the Committee on Bills) to prevent these reaching the floor of the Assembly, he had to instruct the clerk to read two Overtures and a Petition to the house.

The Synod of Angus and Mearns urged the General Assembly to continue to press for abolition, by pursuing the same course of action it had agreed on in 1845. The Synod of Caithness and Sutherland was far more direct. The 'humble Overture' of Angus and Mearns contrasted with a more demanding tone, and certainly more radical message, from the far north of Scotland. They wrote:

That whereas the holding of our fellow-creatures in slavery is inconsistent with the spirit of Christianity, and has,wherever the gospel has been fully preached and its laws acted upon, fallen before it: it is hereby respectfully overtured to the General Assembly, to emit this or a similar declaration; and further, that in any communication that may be held with churches existing in a state which tolerates slavery, to intimate explicitly that this Church cannot continue to hold intercourse

or communication with said Churches, unless they shall be
making open and vigorous efforts for its abolition. [9]
The petition from 'elders, deacons, and other members of the church
in Dundee', the city where Douglass had made such an impact,
called on the Assembly to 'disown fellowship' with those churches
that sanctioned slavery. All this was, however, to be lost in the debate
that followed the latest Candlish report.

Robert Candlish told the Assembly that the Committee had
carefully considered the letter from the Presbyterian Church
of America in response to their 1844 report, and that Church's
deliverances. There was little to report further, except to suggest that
the Committee were not in agreement with some sentiments in the
American document, although it contained 'a clear and unequivocal
disapproval of the system of slavery'. He felt that the only question
before the Assembly was whether the Free Church was justified in
maintaining 'a friendly intercourse' with the American Presbyterian
Church. Not surprisingly he considered that there was only one
answer. Candlish declared that he would not argue the question,
since he did not see that it was open to argument. He then proceeded
to do so at considerable length.

He spoke of 'oneness in the body of Christ' and its catholicity
(universal nature), an argument that he might have hesitated using
to describe relationships in Scotland. He had no regrets that through
circumstances that others might see as unfortunate, the Free Church
had been brought into a relationship with the American church.
He felt that they had much to learn from them, and although he
respected the position of the United Secession Church in declining
further fellowship with the American Presbyterian church, it was far
too early for the Free Church to contemplate that.

He dismissed the petition from Dundee, adding 'I believe the
church and the country know well the circumstances connected with
the getting up of that petition'. Popular clamour, much of it from
outside the church, had, in his view, given the impression that there
was division and confusion in the Free Church on this issue. He
didn't mention Douglass, Buffen and Wright, but they were there by
implication. He received loud applause when he made a rallying cry
to 'stand the clamour of the mob as well as the assaults of the great',
a reference to the circumstances leading to the Disruption.

Candlish then reminded the Free Church that there were many
other issues concerning the American church. He admitted that
their recent position regarding slavery was to be 'deplored' and
'regretted'. But he appealed to the Assembly to put themselves in

the position of the Americans. More tellingly, he argued that to take a stronger line towards them, and put more pressure on to them, might entrench them in their position and even harm 'this great cause of the emancipation of the slave'.

Anticipating that the uncomprising anti-slavery attitude of the late Dr Andrew Thomson would find its way into the debate, Candlish then raised his name. Thomson who, but for his unexpected death in 1831, would have almost certainly have led the Free Church, was a revered figure. In 1830 he had taken up the cause of the immediate abolition of slavery when most were prepared to accommodate to a 'gradual' abolition. For this he had made some enemies in the Church of Scotland, and in the country generally. Candlish pointed out at that at no time did Andrew Thomson contemplate cutting off relationships with the mission churches in the West Indies just because missionaries had to accommodate to slave societies. It was a clever use of a venerated name, but it was somewhat disingenuous. There was a world of difference between the white churches in the United States and the mission stations in the West Indies, which were often attacked by the established churches that the planters attended, and where Thomson was a hated name.

Having reaffirmed the stance of fellowship with the American churches, Candlish became more critical of them. Although the Free Church had left the Church of Scotland in order to assert its spiritual independence, it still saw itself linked through disapproval of those who had adopted 'Voluntarism'.[10] Candlish charged the American Presbyterians of being so influenced by a Voluntarist principle, that they shrank from any engagement with the state on the question of slavery. 'They are too supine', in this regard, he said, although he commended them for the assurance that those who treated slaves as property, not as human beings, would be disciplined by the church.

In the final part of his speech Candlish took a more robust line. He could not countenance any reluctance by the American churches to take an active part in resisting or seeking to change laws that forbad education to slaves, and enabled 'the holy state of marriage' to be violated by the slave-owner dividing families through sales. Candlish fully acknowledged the irony of a nation claiming to stand for freedom, but in many of its parts having laws forbidding people to emancipate their slaves. 'I say', he continued 'that for the church in these circumstances to remain inactive, is a plain and obvious dereliction of duty'.

Candlish then proposed a strange plan. He knew that the negotiation to enable the abolition of slavery by Britain had ended in giving twenty million pounds in compensation to the planters. If America would agree to sell the freedom of its slaves, he affirmed, 'I pledge myself, I pledge my Church, and I pledge the whole country of Scotland, that thousands upon thousands will be poured into America'. Still in a flamboyant mood he wanted to assure the Assembly that slaveholding was *'prima facie* to be viewed as a sin'.

It might then be assumed that the argument made by the abolitionists had been accepted conclusively, but within a few minutes Robert Candlish had switched tack. If a slave-holder presented himself for communion, if he claimed that slave-holding was against his will 'because God in his providence, has been pleased to place him in circumstances in which he has no alternative but to continue a slaveholder or sin', then, for Candlish, that person should not be denied communion. [11] This somewhat subtle, but torturous, use of traditional Calvinist concepts of election and predestination, gave Frederick Douglass a field day later on.

When he had finished, a speaker rose to bring forward a motion. Rev. James Macbeth, minister of Lauriston Free Church, Glasgow was already known as a most implacable opponent of the Free Church policy towards American slavery. The preamble to his motion was peppered with words such as 'accursed system', 'a crime' and 'peculiarly atrocious' in describing slavery. Few in the assembly would disagree so far. But he then spelt out what he regarded as a logical conclusion:

As the American churches had long ago attained to much light on this subject;

> and as this Free Church and many other churches have more than once remonstrated with some of these American churches; this Assembly hearby resolves that this church cannot admit to its pulpits, or to the communion table, any individual in the United States by whom slavery is practiced, nor can receive deputations from any church which does not visit slave-holding members with excommunication; and this resolution this church adopts in the spirit of love towards the churches that are implicated in this sin.[12]

Macbeth argued that many churches had taken this stance, including the Secession and Relief congregations, and the Reformed Presbyterian Church. Given the suspicion of Secessionists and the Voluntary churches within the Free Church as it attempted to gain respectability, this was not perhaps the most persuasive line. Although he argued strongly to limit the Old Testament warrant for slavery to a particular period, and that the Pauline passages on slavery had a very different meaning, his words fell on deaf ears. Despite an impressive quotation from Andrew Thomson which showed clearly that the late venerated minister was uncompromising on the sinfulness of slavery in its 'origin, continuance, effects, and eternally', Macbeth made the mistake of getting into an argument with Candlish over what the latter had or had not said about sin and slave-holding, and ranks closed against him. Candlish in his summing up speech said that he assumed that 'no one is disposed to second the motion made by Mr Macbeth'. And no one was.

Two more major speeches were recorded before the debate was closed. John Duncan, whose fire shown at Edinburgh Presbytery only fifteen months ago had now been doused, indicated that he had been totally convinced by the Candlish position. He made a moral distinction between 'having' a slave and 'holding' a slave, seizing on the illegality of emancipation in many states. Although anyone travelling in the Southern states might find such individuals extremely rare, Duncan posited a scene where an owner wished to free his slaves, even encourage them to run away, but the state would negate any such action by selling them to another owner. He agreed with Candlish that the actions of what he saw as 'extreme abolitionists', did more harm than good, both to the slave and to the cause of abolition to which they all subscribed.[13]

Once again the formidable Dr Cunningham concluded the debate by assuring the Assembly that after all that was said, it was not necessary for him to occupy much of its time. He then expounded on the issue at great length. He took up several of James Macbeth's arguments on scripture and once again made a distinction between the sinfulness of slavery itself and the limited individual culpability of any who happened to be an owner of slaves. Taking up Macbeth's reference, Cunningham refused to allow that any statement by Andrew Thomson could have relevance to the present position, but he did not expand on this.

Perhaps Cunningham's most significant stance was to reject a charge of heresy levelled at the American churches. 'You cannot' he claimed 'convict them of any heresy in regard to their abstract opinions respecting slavery . . . you can only say there is much that is erroneous and defective in their impressions and mode of action'. The interpretation of slavery as a heresy was embraced by a few American churchmen in the North. They were still a small minority, and the leaders of the Free Church had no intention of allying themselves with them.

Dr Cunningham concluded his speech with an assurance that

Great Britain and America, two countries where Christianity was so influential, could not countenance a break in fellowship between each others' churches. 'The absolute unlawfulness', he said, 'of continuing further intercourse' must be 'indisputably shown'. He attacked what he termed 'the ultra-abolitionists', who 'have made it their great business to abuse and calumniate the American Churches'. He may have been thinking of James Macbeth or Henry C. Wright, for both were soft targets; Macbeth because of his isolation in the Assembly, and Wright because of his eccentric and extreme views on drink and the sabbath. Douglass was a tougher enemy to face – he specifically challenged Cunningham's words in speaking to audiences, but he was careful always to keep criticism and satire on the safe side of abuse. The temperature, despite the all but unanimity of the Free Church General Assembly, was rising in the country over a question that would not go away.[14]

A Veteran Abolitionist Enters the Fray

A month before the Assembly, the Glasgow Emancipation Society sent an invitation to William Lloyd Garrison to make another visit to Britain, and received the veteran English abolitionist George Thompson in Scotland. 'We have had a set of glorious meetings here against the Free Church and we are to have more of them this week', wrote Mary Welsh, an Edinburgh resident, but active in the Glasgow society, to her friend Maria Weston Chapman in Boston on 17 May 1846. She continued 'George Thompson, Frederick Douglass, James Buffun and H.C. Wright have done wonders in opening the eyes of the public to this enormous iniquity, never was there such excitement created as at present'.[15]

George Thompson was no stranger to Scotland. A Liverpudlian, he was the first, and one of the very few British abolitionists, to be a professional lecturer on slavery. In 1833 he had helped to found the emancipation societies in Glasgow and Edinburgh while undertaking a series of debates in both cities with Peter Borthwick, an MP who spoke for the interests of the West Indian planters. In 1834 Thompson undertook a speaking tour in America, and after several threats on his life from supporters of slavery, had to flee to Canada. He returned twice to America and served as a radical Member of Parliament from 1847 to 1852.

On 1 May, Thompson introduced Frederick Douglass to an audience of two thousand, who paid six pence each to attend a meeting at the Music Hall in Edinburgh. In his closing speech

Thompson observed that the 'force of public opinion', that had at last 'subdued' West Indian interests, 'need not despair of its influence being felt by Drs Chalmers, Cunningham, and Candlish'. After extensive criticism of Chalmers, he proclaimed that he believed that there was 'still as much manly spirit in the Free Church as would snap the manacles which this clerical triumvirate were fruitlessly endeavouring to impose on the minds of the adherents of their cause'.[16]

After a few weeks in London, Thomson and Douglass returned to Scotland to hear the report of the Candlish Committee to the Free Church General Assembly. When William Cunningham repeated the distinction between slavery as a system and slave-holders, and claimed that the apostles of Jesus 'admitted slave-holders to the table of the Lord', Thompson could not restrain himself from irony. The report of proceedings noted an interruption of 'hear, hear' 'in a very sonorous voice from Mr George Thompson, which for a time raised a slight confusion and interruption'.

When in Edinburgh, Thompson was given the Freedom of the City at the instigation of Duncan Maclaran, a Liberal Councillor, who would be the Lord Provost of Edinburgh in 1851. This was ostensibly for Thompson's advocacy of Free Trade, but it caused fury in the Free Church. For the capital to honour such an outspoken opponent of the church's conduct was certainly an embarrassment to the leadership. A pamphlet was circulated, pointedly entitled *A Review of the Proceedings of a Minority of the Town Council of Edinburgh.* It was reminiscent of the twentieth-century dispute, when Glasgow City Council awarded the Freedom of the City to Nelson Mandela in 1981 while he was still imprisoned on Robben Island.[17]

More specific criticism of Thompson came from Mr. Andrew Cameron, who linked Thompson to Henry C. Wright in arguing that if they had their way, every Christian involved in any way in the American state would be unchurched. [18] As Duncan Rice has pointed out, it was a familiar tactic of Free Church propaganda to link all abolitionists with their most extreme spokesmen.Thompson remained a close friend of Garrison all his life, although he was never a convinced Garristonian.[19] In the meantime Douglass was moving to Ireland and to further conflict with Thomas Smyth.

Chapter 7
Ballads and Broadsheets

Send back the money!- – No; indeed, –
'Tis money is our darling creed
In this ae thing we're all agreed
My faith, we'll keep the money
My Faith we'll keep the Money, 1847

1846 saw a number of broadsheets produced with satirical poems or songs focussing on the Free Church and the contentious money. Not all were sympathetic to the abolitionists, and one formed a crude parody of the perceived 'negro speech' that became the staple of racist variety acts and comics later on in the century. Thomas Chalmers featured prominently, giving substance to Duncan Rice's theory that the 'Send Back the Money' campaign was a convenient stick for other churches to beat the Free Church. Frederick Douglass believed that the broadsheets showed the whole country aflame for the cause. Certainly the songs, set to popular tunes, would have reached the ears of many, but the very few copies that exist today suggest that the script was not mass produced, and the enthusiasm was more limited and certainly less effective than the rhetoric at anti-slavery meetings suggested.

The Cursed Bawbees

The most direct song fitted the tune of one of Robert Burns's most celebrated pieces –'A Man's a Man for a' That'. It was uncompromising and focussed, combining the charge that every piece of money was stained with blood, with the warning that such acceptance brought the curse and the 'avenging rod' of the Almighty on 'Scotland's Church'. No honest man, it argued, could be associated with something gained by 'fraud deceit and shame'. An interesting touch is the mention of 'the negro's God', reminding its listeners that the slaves, who were treated as chattels and objects, were children of the same divine parent. It ends with the direct command to send back the money 'without delay'.

Send back the money, send it back, tis' dark polluted gold
T'was wrang from human flesh and bones by agonies untold
Theres no a mite in a' the sum but what is stained wi' blood
Theres no a mite in a' the sum but what is cursed by God.

Send back the money, send it back, partake not in the sin
Who buy and sell and trade in men, accursed gains to win
Theres no a mite in a' the sum an honest man may claim
Theres no a mite but what can tell of fraud, deceit and shame.

Send back the money, send it back, tempt not the negro's God
To blast and wither Scotland's church wi his avenging rod[1]
Theres no a mite in all the sum but cries to heaven above
For wrath on all who shield the men who trade in negro's blood.

Then send the money back again and send without delay
It may not, must not, cannot bear, the light of British day.

Another popular Scottish tune was 'My Boy David', and a dialogue in broad Scots between Thomas Chalmers and the Free Church was set to this. Chalmers is presented as sitting at a table counting suspicious looking copper coins. Mother Free Church looks at him equally suspiciously and asks where the money came from.

Whaur gat ye the bawbees, my boy Tammy,
Whaur foregather'd ye wi'these, my boy Tammy?
Ah dinna see the thistle blae, the shamrock nor the roses gay.
Sae tell me whaur they cam' frae – I dinna think they're canny.

Chalmers replies with a note of irritation about all the fuss, indicating that if no questions were asked, no lies would be necessary.

Ne'er fash aboot the bawbees, ma kind Mammy;
Speir naething and I'll tell nae lees, ma kind Mammy
I got them as I got the lave, I ask'd ma friens – they freely gave
Sae haud yer tongue and dinna rave. Thir cam frae Indiana.

The song by this time expresses the determination of the Free Church leadership to assert that everything was perfectly in order, with willing friends donating the money. The claim that the money came from the Midwest state of Indiana indicated a need for Chalmers to distance himself from the stigma of colluding with the American South, although that state was one of the most hostile to African Americans in the North. Mother Church, however, simply moves from unease to righteous anger, and indicates the effect that Douglass has had. She is both ashamed of the scandal, and torn by her conscience.

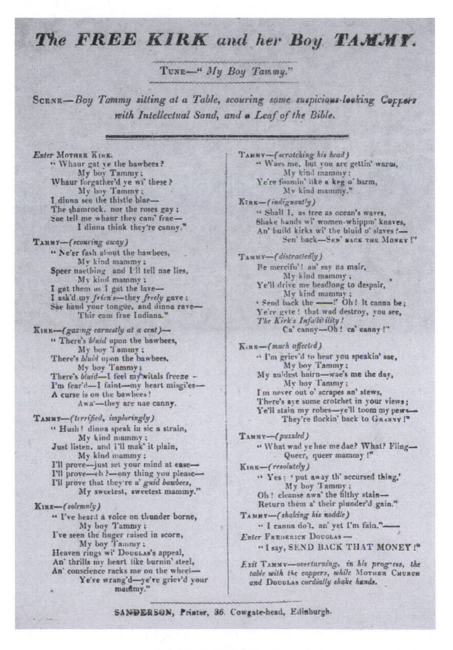

'Send Back the Money' Song

I've heard a voice on thunder borne, my boy Tammy
I've seen the fingers raised in scorn, my boy Tammy
Heaven rings wi' Douglass' appeal,
An' thrills my heart like burning steel
An' conscience racks me on the wheel,
Ye've wranged, ye've grieved yer Mammy.

Chalmers then tries to calm Mother down: 'Ye're foaming like a keg o' barm [beer] my kind Mammy'. But there is no holding back the momentum as she replies:

Shall I, as free as ocean's waves,
Shake hands wi' women whipping knaves[2]
An' build Kirks wi' the bluid o' slaves,
Send back, SEND BACK THE MONEY!

At this 'Tammy' is both torn and worn down by the offensive undertaken by his mother. He replies:

Be mercifu'! and say nae mair, my kind Mammy,
Ye'll drive me headlong to despair, my kind Mammy
"Send back the. . . . Oh! it canna be,
Ye're gyte [mad] that would destroy, ye see,
The Kirk's INFALLIBILITY
Ca' canny [be cautious] – Oh ca' canny.

In the final drama, Mother Kirk accuses Chalmers of polluting her robes by 'the filthy stain' and warns that 'they're flocking back to Granny' (leaving the Free Church to return to the Church of Scotland), but he shakes his head. Douglass enters with the cry 'I say SEND BACK THE MONEY'. Chalmers leaves, overturning the money (a symbol of Jesus overturning the tables of corrupt money changers in the Temple) whilst Douglass and Mother Kirk shake hands.

Clever though the piece is, it greatly exaggerated the opposition to Chalmers and his colleagues within the Free Church – always a small minority in these years. By the same token, despite the popularity of Douglass at large meetings up and down the country, there were very few Free Church ministers, and even members, amongst his adoring followers. Yet this myth of an angry church challenging Chalmers and of his being torn by conscience is reflected in another piece to the tune *Ballenomoro Oro*. One copy advises the reader to sing 'ony [any] tune ye like'. It appeared in the *Montrose Standard* with the introduction about 'that chiel Douglass'. It is headed *The Boy Tammy's Meditations*. The scene, copied from the described broadsheet, is Tammy sitting at a table, scouring some suspicious looking coppers.

(The poet indulgeth in the descriptive)
O Tammy sat laying by his ain fireside
He lookit dumfounered, he groaned and he sighed
   As he shook his lang pow the tears pappan doon
   There will never be peace till that siller's sent hame.

(Moral reflections aboot scouring bluidy bawbees)
I ha'e scoured they bawbees till blabs stan' on ma broo
I may scoor a' ma days, but the bluid aye keeks thro'
I maun e'en sen' them back, just to please oor auld dame
   For she'll no be at peace till that siller's sent hame.

(A case of conscience)
Send it hame?' let me see it gang sair gainst ma hairt
   But its better wi' siller than conscience depairt
   Can we haud be it? Naw, Douglas has blawn sic a flame
   That we winna hae peace till that siller's sent hame

(a Predic')
Its hard, unco hard, to confess we've done wrang
Ane micht do't – but, oh, an *Assembly* ma sang!
But oor folk are uproarious, and cry 'what a shame'
And they'll no gie us peace till that siller's sent hame,

(A dreary prospect)
I ken I've done wrang the world maks sic a din
   Nae smile frae without and nae comfort within
   The deed stamps eternal disgrace on ma name
   And I winna hae peace till that siller's sent hame

(No go)
Thae chiels in Dundee, tho' weel gifted wi' gab,
May talk of the slave-holding patriarch, Job
They may range the hale Bible – it come a' to the same
There'll never be peace till the siller's sent hame

(Random Recollections)
I've played mony a queer pliskie, I trow in my day
I've belauber't Dissenters – weel, weel, let *that gae*
I've run aff frae my Granny, but I've stained my fair fame,
And I'll never hae piece till that siller's sent hame[3]

(A melancholy state of affairs)
Ma mither cries, 'Tammy, correct the mistak-
   As usual there's Patterraw John at ma back;[4]

While 'The Slave' redds ma hair wi' his murderous kaim
And'll no be at peace till that siller's sent hame.

(Ah Tam! Ah Tam!)
Ma mither, pair buddy, shares a' ma disgrace
Wi a tear in her ee she aye glowers in ma face
She gangs aboot dowie and greetin for shame
She'll no give me peace till the siller's sent hame.

(Tammy jocosely addresses himself)
Aye Tammy ma man you've a will o' yer ain
To retract een a hairsbreadth ah ken gives ye pain
But ah doot ye maun do it tho' twoud coup ilka scheme
For there'll never be peace till the siller's sent hame.

(Visions)
Wi' a heartrendin' sigh, and a shak' o'his head
Tammy, sairly preplext, slippit aff till his bed
But he raved in his sleep, and cried oot in his drame
THERE'LL NEVER BE PEACE TILL THAT SILLER'S
SENT HAME,

Making Money on Both Sides

A more realistic view of the collusion of the Free Church was
expressed in the song *Guid Luck to Oor Coffers*. This one recognises
the effect that George Thompson's speeches had and accepts that the
money is not going to be returned.

Have ye heard what a stir Thompson's made in our toon
Aboot the Free Church's American boon
The slaveholders were pleased wi' the cunning game
played
They came doon with their dollars, the priest weighed
his prayers.
Then O for guid luck to oor coffers
Then O for guid luck to oor coffers
Then O for guid luck to oor coffers
There[s some yellow guineas for me.

Ma worthedy priest[5] was pleased to allow
That a' the slaveholders were Christians now
Ma doctor he blessed them for what they had paid
And wished them success in their slaveholding trade
Then O for guid luck to oor coffers etc.

> But the great Free Kirk leaders are men of renown
> It's not public clamour will ere put them down
> Tae send back the money they'll lend a deaf ear
> And fondly caress all their ill gotten gear
> Then O for guid luck to oor coffers etc.

One piece that parodied the dispute between Chalmers and Douglass in the satire of eccentric prose by Dody Tomkins, whose full title was *'The Yankee Looking Glass' or 'Measure for Measure' containing a report of the speeches delivered at a Disorderly Meeting held on Friday last in the Music Hall with a letter from Tomkins to his friends in Edinburgh in Affliction*. Much of it, as mentioned earlier, was an attack on Henry C. Wright and James Buffen, but inserted in the middle of a disconnected diatribe was this rhyme based on a children's jingle, with the words 'sow's erse' replaced by a more acceptable alternative:

> Chalmy and Blackie ran a race
> Chalmy fell and broke his face
> Quo' Blackie I have won the race
> And the sow's tail till him yet
> And the sow's tail till him yet
> And the sow's tail to Chalmy

Thompson and Douglass feature in a clever if crude parody on the abolitionists, thought to have been written by students at New College, the Free Church divinity college in Edinburgh. It casts Thompson in the light of a mercenary, and although Douglass is scripted with the racist stereotypical speech of an African, he is demanding his just share of the profits of anti-slavery lecturing. The piece is entitled *Send Back the Money – A New Version* and published in June 1846. The scene begins with Thompson alone at a table which is covered with papers. He has a £50 note in his hand and muses:

> Ah, this is good! They pay right well;
> Who would not time and talent sell;
> Who would not every scruple quell,
> To sail my boat
> Let truth be hiding in her well,
> I like this note.
>
> I've trimmed my sail in many a tack,
> But Douglas, my imported black
> And this of '*Send the money back*'
> The best perhaps;
> They'll fill my pockets in a crack,
> Th'Established chaps.

I've played the d-v-l with the Frees,
'Tis true I think the others geese
But willingly they furnish grease
To oil my cry.
The cause (I only want the fees)
Is all my eye.

Douglas then enters 'on tip-toe, his finger at his nose, and winking his left eye'. He begins:

Ah! Massa Thompson, what you 'tink?
I hear'd de sound of Money's clink,
So widoub noise I in did slink;
What hab you dere?
A leetle nod's as good's a wink;
Come share and share!

Thompson 'hastily secreting the £50 note' responds:

Ah *Mister* Douglas, my dear friend!
How do you do? You may depend
Upon it that *we'll* make them send
The money back
You'll be a great man in the end
Although you're black. [6]

Douglas replies, 'Pale [sic] with rage'

I want de money back from you
I don't care what the Free Church do;
I saw de note, and hear'd you too,
I do declare.
Dat you must keep your promise true,
And gib me share

Thompson reluctantly gives Douglass a £20 note, 'Of course, dear Douglass! Theres the tin' and after his departure shows what the writer feels are his true motives.

I wish the slave were back again
No wonder the Free folks retain
The cash – alack!
It costs an awful lot of pain
To give it back.

There are three other poems/songs on broadsheets printed by Sanderson of Edinburgh.

The most telling points in favour of not returning the money were contained in a poem by R.H., entitled *O don't send back the money'*. It was a familiar charge against the campaigns to abolish slavery, that scant attention was given to the plight of the poor in Britain. The prose is accompanied by a picture of a slave in chains. The first verse objects:

> The people cry about starvation
> Yet say 'send the money back'.
> Give us poor people back the blunt
> And we'll soon make it play smack.

R.H. then suggests that to return the money would make the slave-owners angry, leading to 'sorer sharper strokes, upon the poor slave's back'. However, since it is said to be 'the price of blood, and groanings of the black' he suggests that the question should be put to the slave.

> Why would the nigger thus reply?
> To answer I'll not be slack –
> "Our massa's got enough just now
> So don't sent it them back."
> Yes, their masters have it to the full,
> While we it sorely lack;
> So pop't to us like fellows good,
> And do not send it back.
> Three thousand is indeed no go –
> How foolish 'tis to talk
> 'Bout sending it to Yankee land –
> Oh do not send it back.

It may be that this was in fact an ironic attack on the Free Church position. There could be no such doubt about the other two. *My Faith. We'll Keep the Money* spells out the accusation of hypocrisy. There is a sideswipe against Chalmers (strangely termed 'north country Tam') in verse three, 'the twa three mair' is a reference to Drs Cunningham and Candlish, and in the last verse there is a none too hidden aping of Burns's *A Man's a Man for 'a that*:

> Send back the money! – No; indeed, –
> 'Tis money is our darling creed
> In this ae thing we're all agreed
> My faith, we'll keep the money.

> If a' the slaves were stanin' there,
> Their woolly heads and shouthers bare,
> For their dark souls we'd mak a prayer
> But faith, we'll keep the money.

> 'Tis nae use for to try and cram
> Our leader true, north country Tam;
> To haud the grip he is nae sham, –
> My faith, he'll keep the money.

> There's twa three mair (ye ken them weel)
> Wha're bless'd wi' nerves an' hearts o' steel,
> They'd mak a compact wi' the de'il
> E'er they'd send back the money
>
> O money! Source of a' our joy
> It does our noblest pow'rs employ
> That is a theme can never cloy
> Come, gi'e the Free Kirk money.

Sanderson's third broadsheet featured an old Free Church member telling his wife that they were returning to the Church of Scotland because, as he put it, 'you have only to pay for your seat, and they ask for nae mair o' your siller'.[7] The old man is well aware that there is an issue here but is irritated by the constant financial appeals as witness these two verses:

> Losh! Kate, I hae gotten some news;
> The Free Kirk there're fairly set till her;
> They're hounding her like a wheen grouse,
> An' they say she maun send back the siller
>
> Ev'ry week they have got some new scheme
> (How can they thin folk will stick till her?)
> Ye hear naething ava but the name,
> An' they ask you for mair o' your siller,

The Stain of Slaveholders' Money

As we have seen, Thomas Chalmers was at great pains to excuse slave-owning (or 'slave-holding' as he put it) on the grounds that it could be a status in life that was divinely ordained. The special iniquity of slave-owning clergy was not lost on the abolitionists, who gave full vent to this in the song *Complaint of Minister's Slave*, published and printed by J. Fairgrieve and Co. of Rose Street, Edinburgh.

The explanation was caustic. 'The first mentioned', it read, 'found himself placed in the unhappy predicament of a Slaveholder or haver by God's Providence'. A sample of its verses tells the tale of his abuse and that of his wife who is sold to benefit 'The Free' (Church).

> I'm poor; the highest wage I got
> For all my toil and pain,
> Was blows and stripes from morn till night
> The collar and the chain.
>
> These eyes that now with care are dim,

Have seen my master's lash
Sink deep into the quivering limb
And the blood stream from the gash.

I was too happy for a slave –
Upon one fatal day
My wife and child were torn from me
And parted far away
My master gave my love! My life!
For gold, for cursed gold; –
For silks and jewels for his wife
My only child he sold!

When they were gone some white men came
From a land beyond the sea;
They took away the price of blood,
And gave it to the FREE!!!

White stranger, if thou hast a heart,
For white men here have none.
Return into thy slaveless land
And tell the deeds here done

Tell there of all our bloody tears,
Our every groan and sigh,
 Tell that no Bible e'er was here
To speak of God on high
Three millions of thy fellow-men
Will bless you ere they die

To which is added:

Hush! Says the Reverend double D.[8]
These impious feeling smother
Your master is a holy man
A *(blank)* Church Christian Brother!!!

An anonymous poem, *The Sighs of the Slave*, contained an appeal to
the Free Church to return to its heritage, and invoked John Knox and
Andrew Thomson:

O spirit of Knox! art thou slumbering now
When such a dark stain is affixed to thy brow
And oh! Thomson thou eloquent friend of the slave,
Awaken and lift thy lone head from the grave.

Tell the Free Church of Scotia, bright star of the North
All resplendent with intellect, talent and worth,

'Tis in vain she abhors slave oppression and toils
While she shares in the guilt of its blood purchased spoils.

The end result

When Frederick Douglas wrote to his Dublin abolitionist friend,
Richard Webb, with such enthusiasm about the boys in the streets
singing songs about sending the money back, he was almost
certainly over egging the pudding. But he was not the only one. At
a meeting in London in May 1846 George Thompson described the
verbal attack on the Free Church position in equally dramatic terms.
'People come to us' said Thompson:

> Literally weeping over the error that has been committed
> by the deputation. They are singing songs in the streets of
> Scotland 'Send Back the Money'. They are writing on the
> walls of the Free Church 'Send Back the Money' and when a
> gentleman with a black coat and a white kerchief [presumably
> a Free Church minister] passes through the streets, a little
> child whispers 'Send Back the Money'.[9]

Yet the anti-slavery songs of 1846 and 1847 probably reached only
a fraction of those who were struck by the oratory of Douglass,
Thompson, and other speakers at the mass meetings during that
time. They were akin to satirical pieces today in *Punch* or even
Private Eye. Cleverly crafted and hard hitting though they were, and
interesting for later generations to read, there was a huge chasm
between them and the songs and poetry of protest enduring in the
folklore of Scotland, let alone Ireland.

In recent years there has been a rediscovery of the hidden layer of
what used to be called 'negro spirituals', with codes built into them
to indicate either the longing for escape from slavery, or indeed
the practical guidelines. Canaan's land was code for Canada where
slavery from 1834 was illegal. 'Steal away to Jesus' which seemed to
a slave-owner to be a 'harmless' pious expression, was of course a
signal for a silent night-time flight from the plantation. The veteran
self-liberated slave Harriet Tubman, who made many trips back to
the south to rescue others, was famed for singing 'spirituals' which
held hidden messages for those in hiding in the fields.

Compared with this, the Scottish anti-slavery offerings of the
1840s seem very thin and unenduring. But they should not be
discounted. The authors often displayed a detailed knowledge of
who or what was prominent in the cause during that time – John
Ritchie and George Thompson feature, in addition to Frederick

Douglass, although invoking the spirit of John Knox alongside that
of Andrew Thomson in the service of abolitionism was going too far.
Knox had himself been captured by the French, and had briefly been
pressed into service as a 'galley slave' by them exactly three hundred
years previously.

Probably the most that can be claimed for these pieces, was
that they helped to keep the issue before the public at that time. In
company with many other causes of agitation it reflected very real
bitterness towards the Free Church from other denominations, but
that did not mean that this was the dominant agenda. Certainly the
'Send Back the Money' campaign produced a few verbal and other
cudgels with which to belabour the Free Church, and in particular
Thomas Chalmers, but that was not its only, or even its prime,
purpose. Within the songs and poems of that time are few enduring
gems. But there is an honest, and sometimes crude, passion that comes
through, and an underlying humanity. In 1778, a decade before the
first petitions against the slave trade were sent to Parliament, judges
in Scotland's highest court decided by a majority that Scotland's law
could not support slavery, and freed a man brought from Jamaica
to Perthshire.[10] One of them, the father of James Boswell, simply
based his decision on his feeling that to hold a man in bondage
was not right or Christian. Throughout the long history of Scottish
involvement with slavery and anti-slavery over several centuries,
despite so much cruelty and exploitation by Scots abroad, there has
always been a basic streak of deep-seated revulsion to inhumanity.

Chapter 8
The Irish take a Firmer Stand

As Mr. Douglass has taken the most unwarrantable liberties with my name, even before my coming to this country, &, not merely attempted to injure me deeply in public opinion, but has so far succeeded as to enable me to prove, if desirable, special damage...I shall therefore in self-defence feel bound to appeal against him to the laws of my native country, and teach him to respect the characters of others while he is so sensitively – &, I, will add, justly, most chary of his own.
> Rev. Dr Thomas Smyth to Messrs Davison and Torrens, Solicitors, 17 July 1846

Douglass in Ireland

Before touring Scotland, Frederick Douglass had made an extensive speaking tour in Ireland from August 1845 to January 1846. In Dublin he stayed with the Quaker Garrisonian Richard Webb, Secretary of the Hibernian Anti-Slavery Society.[1] The Dublin paper, *Evening Packet and Correspondent* on 4 October reported that he 'riveted the attention of his hearers by his eloquent appeals on behalf of his outraged coloured brethren'. The title of his address 'Irish Christians and Non-Fellowship with Man Stealers' set the tone. In Cork he explained how 'Slavery corrupts American Society and Religion'. As in Scotland Douglass took advantage of the strong Irish Temperance Movement, being introduced in Cork on 20 October by the veteran anti-slavery priest, Father Theobald Mathew, as 'a consistent and faithful teetotaller' and proclaimed that 'if we could make the world sober we would have no slavery'.

From the West of Ireland Douglass journeyed to Belfast in early December 1845, and spoke of his experiences as a slave. At Donegal Street Church, two days before Christmas, Douglass raised the issue of the Free Church of Scotland being 'implicated' in 'the crime of slavery'. In arguing that the Northern churches colluded with slavery, he compared Rev. Dr Daniel Sharp from Boston with Dr

Slave Auction in Richmond, Virginia

Chalmers as they both looked 'on slavery as an evil, that though wrong in itself, nevertheless, is not important enough to exclude persons from Christian Union'.[2]

A letter from Douglass to Garrison published in *The Liberator* on 20 March 1846 spoke of 'the entire absence of everything that looked like prejudice against me, on account of the color of my skin'. That may have been so overall, but it was more true of the largely Roman Catholic south than in the north. The Belfast Anti-Slavery Society gave a breakfast in his honour in early January 1846, where he was presented with a gold-bound pocket Bible inscribed with a message of 'respect and esteem for his personal character', and presented him with $200, in addition to covering his stay at the Victoria Temperance Hotel. Mary Ireland, one who was captivated by Douglass, wrote to her friend Maria Weston Chapman, the celebrated Boston abolitionist, that there was 'scarcely a lady in Belfast' whom he had not convinced to join the anti-slavery crusade.

However, it was not all one way traffic. Mary's letter to Maria spoke also of those who normally 'take the lead in other good works', yet were 'offended by the uncompromising tone of Mr Douglass in regard to the Free Church of Scotland' and saw them as 'either avowed enemies to the present movement or very hollow friends'. Just as Douglass was himself to encourage in Scotland, placards and street cries rang out in Belfast in 1846. This time instead of 'Send Back the Money', the slogan was all too often 'Send back the Nigger'. Even his friend Richard Webb, writing to Maria Chapman in February 1846, said that H.C. Wright had told him Douglass was 'making money hand over head' and that he (Webb) had 'met with insolence from him' (Douglass), that had been caused by 'headiness induced by the flattery and petting he met with in his travels in Ireland'. The Webb/Weston correspondence came to Douglass's notice, and in March 1846 he complained to Maria that 'you betray a want of confidence in me as a man, and an abolitionist, utterly inconsistent with all the facts in the history of my connection with the Anti-Slavery Movement'.[3]

The native son returns

The great waves of emigration from Ulster to America in the eighteenth and early nineteenth century ensured that Irish Presbyterians were well represented in the United States. Cordial relationships had existed with the sister churches, and Thomas Smyth of Charleston had been born in Lurgan and educated in Belfast. He had kept up his contacts with close friends in the Irish Presbyterian Church, one of whom was later to turn against him. In 1846 Smyth crossed the Atlantic once more with two aims in mind. The first was to help settle the estate of his late aunt, Mrs Margaret Magee of Dublin, who had left in excess of £100,000 to the Presbyterian Church in Ireland. The second was to attend the international gathering in London of the Evangelical Alliance, which was to see severe ructions over the issue of slavery later that year.[4]

Thomas Smyth's visit to Ireland in 1846 was to prove a touchstone for the Presbyterian Church's attitude to the American Church and slavery. He entered these stormy Irish waters and immediately felt under attack. By a strange coincidence, he and Frederick Douglass both crossed the Irish sea in the same month of July. Smyth claimed that he had never heard of Douglass, but that was soon to change. Already those whom he had seen as friends and allies seemed to have been persuaded to join Douglass's cause. Robert Bell, a boyhood friend, who had given Smyth a testimonial when he went to America, had organised the Belfast Auxiliary Female Anti-Slavery Society, which was inspired by Douglass's oratory. In January 1846, Mary Cunningham, whose meeting with him in Belfast in 1844 led her to address him as 'your affectionate friend and fellow traveller', wrote to him in profound distress, having heard from Douglass that 'slave-owners are admitted to communion', and even worse that 'ministers of "the gospel" hold their fellow creatures in this state of frightful bondage'.[5]

What Smyth didn't fully realise was that in 1845 the Irish Presbyterian Church had taken a much more robust line over the slavery issue with American Presbyterians than had the Free Church of Scotland. Dr Isaac Nelson of Donegal Street Church in Belfast, later to become a radical Irish Member of Parliament and Home Ruler, had encouraged the Free Church Anti-Slavery Society, and tried hard to persuade the Irish Presbyterians to cut links with the Americans. Nelson, like Bell, was an enthusiast for Douglass. At the end of a series of lectures given by Douglass in Belfast in January 1846, Nelson declared that the American was 'raised up by God to do a great work'. At the same time Nelson himself was known to be 'daggers drawn' with most of his ministerial colleagues on a wide range of issues. He was a powerful advocate of an uncompromising position over slavery but he was unlikely to win over many of his colleagues because his reputation produced an instant reaction.

After the 1846 Assembly, Nelson wrote to the *Northern Whig* that the Assembly had said that there should be 'no fellowship with slaveholders', who as 'man stealers' were condemned in scripture as 'sinners of the worst description', and that this was why the Irish Assembly refused to let Smyth sit in it. He quoted a member of the Assembly, who argued 'we can have no communion with a church advocating the system of slavery', and added himself: 'The Free Church will be obliged to take a more scriptural view of the whole question'.

Smyth's own account in his memoirs give a different interpretation. 'My friends' he wrote:

Found that the introduction of my name into the Assembly would lead to excitement and unpleasant remarks and, by my request, withheld it. It was therefore advertised in the Unitarian paper, the *News Letter*, that Rev. Dr. Smyth, in his own native city, among his own friends, notwithstanding his high reputation and connections, was excluded from a seat in the house and that the sexton was instructed to exclude me as a slaveholder, all of which was an abolition lie after the usual order.

The previous year Smyth had been recommended by Dr James Reid, historian of the Irish Presbyterians, for an Honorary Degree at Glasgow University. As the process was going through, Reid died, and his professorial son by contrast advised the University to be wary of honouring a Southern supporter of slavery. The matter was dropped, and in his memoirs Smyth expressed his conviction that 'the agitation' of Frederick Douglass had led to this.

Before crossing to Ireland Smyth had stopped off in Edinburgh, and shortly afterwards became embroiled in a correspondence with Rev. James Robertson, Secretary of the newly formed Scottish Anti-Slavery Society.[6] Robertson thought that he was still staying at the Regent Hotel in Waterloo Place, and invited him to a engage in public debate with Frederick Douglass, Henry C. Wright, James Buffen, 'any or all of these gentlemen', to prove to the public that any statement regarding himself or 'the religious party to which you belong' in the matter of slavery, to be, as Smyth claimed, 'unfounded'.

Smyth replied that he was prepared to defend his allegation that the statements of the abolitionists were unfounded, but saw no value in public discussion, that would inevitably in his view 'injure the cause of Christ, the amelioration of slavery, and the best interests of the slaves themselves'. The tempo rose with each letter. On 6 July Robertson, riled by Smyth's criticism of the veteran English abolitionist George Thompson, went on to defend his character as a man 'known in both hemispheres as the true friend of the human race'. Compared with that, said Robertson, what 'is publically known about you' in Scotland was 'all against you'. Strangely he inaccurately attributed to Smyth a Scottish birth, and continued by holding him responsible for the innocent blood of slaves. 'You are an accused and suspected man' wrote Robertson:

> You are considered a recreant Scotsman and an unfaithful minister of Jesus Christ; forget not that you come from Charleston, South Carolina – the land where men and women are degraded to the level of brutes – where the prerogative of God is invaded, and where an interdict is put on the Commission of the Saviour to preach the gospel to every creature – where the laws of the Eternal one are trampled underfoot, and where might not right is the rule of action for persons who claim to be followers of Jesus Christ; keep in mind that with these atrocities you are either directly or indirectly identified. And when you have reflected a little say to yourself- my place is to be humble and contrite.

With that kind of polemic there was of course no possibility of any dialogue, and Robertson's suggestion that the Society might arrange a public debate with Smyth, a remote possibility at any time, was finally and firmly buried deep. Understandably, Smyth accused Robertson of 'invading the prerogative of the Deity', in judging his spirit and motives. The correspondence rattled furiously, rather than rumbled on, into the late summer. On 11 August Robertson described Smyth's last response as 'sanctimonious' and 'vain'. 'It is more than vain', he wrote, 'it is *impious* to refer to the revelation of the blessed God as you do, as if it has contained a single line to authorise the *villainy* and doing wrong of the *man stealers*'.[7]

Libel and Defamation

Such an exchange in the end petered out. Far more serious was the issue that had led to correspondence between Smyth and Douglass between 9 and 11 July. Douglass had learnt that Smyth had accused the abolitionist of being 'an infidel', and that he had been seen coming out of a brothel in Manchester. These statements, were supposed to have been made to Smyth by an Irish minister Rev. Mr. McCurdy, and, more bizarrely, by Rev. Joshua Himes from Boston, described as 'an immediate abolitionist'. Douglass wrote to Smyth about the matter, but claimed to have received no satisfaction. In the meantime, Smyth was visited by his old friend Robert Bell and his less cordial fellow minister Isaac Nelson, who both asked for evidence of the charges or retraction.

Richard Webb had heard of these reports and wrote to Maria Weston Chapman:

> In Belfast a Carolinian Rev. Smith, a Methodist, endeavoured
> to injure Douglass by calumnious reports against his morality
> and by imputing infidelity to him. One night the town was
> placarded with large bills *Send Back the Nigger*. This could have
> come from nobody but this diabolical 'minister of Christ'.

Smyth certainly was to own up to the first charge, but Webb's sloppiness in failing to recognise Smyth's denominational allegiance calls the rest of the statement into question. Angered as he was by Douglass's hostility to him, it is too fanciful to imagine him organising a counter campaign of such crude racist posters.

Pressure was mounting on Thomas Smyth. His final break from Robert Bell came on 16 July when the latter denounced him and turned his back on their former friendship, withdrawing his offer of hospitality at his manse. 'From what I knew of you', wrote Bell:

> Your conduct in relation to Douglass, a poor fugitive slave,
> in retailing and circulating vile hearsay calumnies against
> him, and the fact of Rev. Mr McCurdy totally denying the
> statements you imputed to him, leaves me at a loss to know
> what to think.

'Fugitive slave' Douglass might still have been, subject to re-enslavement had he been anywhere near Smyth's Charleston, but for the moment he was the one making the running. On the same day Smyth received a letter from the Belfast solicitors, Davison and Torrens, acting on behalf of Frederick Douglass, commencing an action for libel and seeking a writ to hold Smyth in the country. He immediately replied, hoping that a lawsuit would be avoidable, but pledging his word to remain in contact from Dublin, where he would be. He claimed that he had himself never made these statements, but only repeated the words of the two others.

These 'others' seemed to be somewhat elusive witnesses. Joshua Himes was confused with the name Hynes and appeared to be in England. Rev. Mr McCurdy's other names or location seemed to be unknown to him. The whole incident became farcical when he identified several McCurdy's, who denied all knowledge of him, let alone the statements made. The Rev. Samuel McCurdy told Smyth in a letter of 25 July that he was not 'the right McCurdy', but wished Smyth well, after a fashion. Whilst satisfied at Smyth's apology for using his name incorrectly he added:

> Permit me jocularly to say that your return to Irish ground seems to have exerted an influence not unfriendly to Irish Blundering, for you address me at Co. Kerry, which is rather remote from Co. Tyrone where I reside. Wishing you safely out of the scrape, I am Revd Sir, yours respectfully.

After scouring Ireland, Thomas Smyth located the right McCurdy, who was actually a John McCourdie. By that time it was too late to do anything and he had retracted.

Despite the advice on 23 July of McDowell Elliott, his own Belfast solicitor, not to be hurried into statements that would allow 'the Douglass party' to 'hold up any unnecessary apology or retraction as a triumph', Smyth had been minded to close the issue immediately. On 17 July he had written to Douglass's lawyers recognising that they had been instructed to institute proceedings against him 'for certain statements made by me injurious to his moral and religious character', and begging to:

> Express my sincere regret for having uttered the same: the more especially as, on mature reflection, I am quite satisfied that the statement I incautiously made on the report of the third parties were unfounded.

Smyth, probably out of weariness, and now very bruised, could not forbear to add that if the letter which Davison and Torrens were drawing up was 'unsatisfactory to Mr. Douglass', then he had to add:

> As Mr. Douglass has taken the most unwarrantable liberties with my name, even before my coming to this country, &, not merely attempted to injure me deeply in public opinion, but has so far succeeded as to enable me to prove, if desireable, special damage. . . . I shall therefore in self-defence feel bound to appeal against him to the laws of my native country, and teach him to respect the characters of others while he is so sensitively – &, I, will add, justly – most chary of his own.

These were hardly the words of a typical white southerner to a man who was technically still a slave. Douglass must have recognised that and his lawyers in turn wrote to Smyth on 21 July indicating that they were enclosing a form of apology for him to sign which he did. They stated in the letter that Mr Douglass had no 'vindictive feelings to gratify'. Nevertheless, on 30 July Douglass wrote to an American friend: 'I am playing the mischief with the character of slaveholders in this land. Rev. Thomas Smyth of Charleston has been kept out of every pulpit here. I think I have been partly the means of it. He is terrible mad with me for it'.

Smyth has been described by his biographer Erskine Clarke as a 'moderate Southerner'. His attitude to slaves was paternalistic, and he desperately sought a middle ground on slavery, which was becoming increasingly untenable. What must have bitterly hurt him, was the title given to him of 'slave-holder', not least by Douglass. Although he defended the rights of those who did, Thomas Smyth claimed that he 'was not a slave-holder or haver personally' (a strange distinction that Chalmers had used to justify the Free Church position) and that he had no 'pecuniary interest in the system'. When this was pointed out to Douglass, the abolitionist claimed that this was pretence. In a speech in Edinburgh on 24 September 1846 Douglass stated that 'he [Smyth] some time ago married a wife [Margaret Adger of Charleston] and thus became possessed of slaves, though he always says that it is his wife who holds them'. This brought laughter from his audience, but as with many of the charges hurled between abolitionists and those defending slavery, the facts were hard to establish – the rhetoric much easier to offer.

Thomas Smyth remained on good terms with some of his old Presbyterian contacts, but he had suffered some humiliating experiences in Ireland. It was true that his name had not been painted on walls in Ireland, as his brother-in-law John Adger informed him was the case in Scotland.[8] But the tide was running much stronger in his native land towards conflict with the slave-churches of America, as characterised by the correspondence that year.

Assemblies and letters to America

The issue of fellowship with slave-owners had surfaced in the Presbyterian Church in Ireland some time before the Free Church of Scotland delegation set off for America. In 1841 Dr James Morgan, Minister of Fisherwick Presbyterian Church in Belfast, addressed the Belfast Anti-Slavery Society, and raised the issue of 'non-fellowship' with slave-owners. The following year, at the General Assembly of the Presbyterian Church, Dr John Edgar, Professor of Theology in Belfast, encouraged the delegates from the Moderator's chair, to 'remonstrate with their American brethren on the subject of slavery'. Although many commissioners were concerned that brother Presbyterians seemed to engage on behalf of the slave system, the highly respected Dr Henry Cooke, leader of the evangelical group, persuaded the Assembly to depart from the issue, which he claimed was a 'political matter'.[9]

Shortly afterwards relations between abolitionists and the Irish Presbyterians took a turn for the worse with the arrival of Henry C. Wright at the end of 1844. Wright was warned by the Belfast Anti-Slavery Society not to attack the free Church of Scotland. Inevitably he ignored that, and managed to alienate just about every Presbyterian minister, except Isaac Nelson, whose Church was the only one willing to host him. Wright did, however, gain some support from Independents and Reformed Presbyterians. How much of this was enthusiasm for Wright's fervency in the anti-slavery cause, or his distaste for any ecclesiastical or civic organisation, and how much it was to thumb their noses at the dominant Presbyterians, is hard to gauge. It alienated John Edgar, who refused to condemn the Free Church publically, and was himself condemned by Isaac Nelson.

Transatlantic communication in the mid nineteenth-century could be painfully slow, as the churches were to find out. The 1845 General Assembly of the Irish Presbyterians had agreed, and sent, a letter of concern over slavery to the Americans, but the reply, dated 27 May, had not only arrived too late for the summer Assembly to respond, but was received in Belfast in the middle of October. It did, however, give the Committee set to correspond with 'Foreign Churches', plenty of time to draft and revise a text in the light of 1846 Assembly and to forward it to America in July of that year.

On the first day of the 1846 Assembly, the new Moderator, Dr James Morgan, described the American response as 'containing the usual defence' of slavery. The bulk of the response, in his view, consisted of attacks on the abolitionists. Isaac Nelson argued that a stronger remonstrance should be sent immediately. Henry Cooke argued for non-interference. The Assembly asked a Committee to draft a reply, and to bring it before them again.

The Committee produced two possible letters. The first stopped short of refusing fellowship, but warned that their brethren were 'guilty before God'. The second was much stronger, and urged them to expel from communion anyone who refused to free their slaves, expressing the conviction that no Christian church could hold fellowship with those who held slaves or 'winked' at slavery. The letter that was sent in the end was a compromise between the two. Isaac Nelson consulted with Scottish abolitionists and had it printed and distributed in Scotland, mainly to counteract *The Witness*, which was arguing that the Free Church and Irish Presbyterian Church were of the same mind over the issue.

The 1846 letter to America began with heartfelt thanksgiving that the threat of war between Britain and America over the territory of Oregon had been averted, and emphasised the need to cultivate friendly relations between countries which had so many ties in common. The Assembly noted 'with much pleasure the frankness and good feeling which you manifest when alluding to our remonstrances on the subject of slavery'. The preamble continued: 'we pretend to no superiority and assume no authority over our brethren in America, but we feel it our duty, on the present occasion, to take the liberty, in all kindness, of expressing more fully our views of the American slave system'.

That last statement already took the issue further than the Free Church Assembly's communication with the Presbyterian Church in America. It then gave licence to raise questions that the Candlish Commission in Scotland had refused to do.

The first was the obvious one. 'You appear proud of the liberty which the inhabitants of the United States enjoy', said the letter, continuing, 'permit us to ask when your hearts are buoyant with the triumphant feeling of conscious liberty, what must the bitter experience of the poor slave in America, who is as much the property of his master as his ox or his ass, and who has no liberty but to submit, suffer, and obey'.

The Free Church of Scotland had condemned slavery as a general system, but it was Douglass who brought to Scottish audiences the personal aspects that had been absent from official Scottish Church communications. The Irish Presbyterians continued by using the phrase 'man stealers' beloved by abolitionists, and only heard from dissenters from the Free Church position.

The Irish Presbyterians went on to challenge their American brethren, who had stated their abhorrence of 'traffic in slaves for the sake of gain', to follow that up by doing all 'as far as in you lies' to stop it. They then asked whether any slaveholder who refused their slaves the use of scripture or Christian instruction would be allowed to remain members of the Church, affirming that 'the Lord and his apostles would not have acknowledged as disciples any who under any name or pretence, were guilty of such wickedness'.

The Irish refused to follow their Free Church brethren in hiding behind the laws of the Slave States, many of whom made the teaching of slaves illegal. Instead they quoted the Acts of the Apostles, 'we are to obey God rather than men'. No amount of disapproval, they wrote, would be of any use at all, 'if you admit to Christian privileges any who support by their practice such cruel and unscriptural enactments'.

The Assembly recognised that the opposition to the abolitionists in the Southern churches of America far outweighed the opposition to those 'who are seeking to perpetuate the accursed system of American bondage'. Keeping to the most blatant example of anti-Christian behaviour on slavery, the letter pointed out the hypocrisy of the American enthusiasm for mission overseas, whilst the slavery system keeps 'so many in a state of deplorable heathenism at home'.[10]

Despite Isaac Nelson and Robert Bell's best efforts, the Assembly had stopped short of a threat to disassociate themselves from the American Presbyterians. In fact there had been opposition in the Assembly to sending the letter at all. Nelson's assertion in the *Northern Whig* that the Assembly said that there should be 'no fellowship with slaveholders', took the penetrating challenges in the July letter to a level that was more reflective of his position than the Assembly's. What both had succeeded in doing, had been to prevent Thomas Smyth from exercising any voice in Ireland and ensured that the dominant one was that of Frederick Douglass.

There was a sharp response from the American Presbyterians which the 1847 Assembly received. It reaffirmed the position which had earlier received support from Thomas Chalmers, that slavery was a civil, and not an ecclesiastical, matter. In a fairly blatant disregard for the issue of humanity, which at least the Free Church had emphasised, the Americans compared the Irish position with the hypothetical one of their attempting to interfere with the British monarchy. That of course was neatly inserted to cause ripples amongst Northern Irish Protestants, as was the comment that there were 'millions enslaved by Popery', and the church would be better to concentrate on that in their own back yard.[11]

There were many ministers in the Presbyterian Church in Ireland deeply anxious that Frederick Douglass and other abolitionists from outside were dangerous fanatics, who would discredit the church. Although the Belfast Anti-Slavery Committee had been energised over this period, the same pattern emerged as in Scotland with clergy of the smaller denominations being the most active. Isaac Nelson and James Morgan were the only Presbyterian Church ministers on its Committee and the *Northern Whig*, the newspaper most supportive of the abolitionists, blamed what they called 'this smooth parson' (Morgan) for supposed backtracking on slavery.

Given all this, it was remarkable that the Irish Presbyterian Assembly managed to take a much firmer line towards the Americans than the Free Church. Douglas Riach has pointed out that the Presbyterians were caught between not wanting to break off relationships with the Free Church of Scotland, and not wanting to appear to be seen as weak on slavery. For that reason Thomas Smyth was an embarrassment to them.

The answer is probably that the establishment had no great figures – Henry Cooke was certainly one, but he withdrew from that role in the Assembly due to his disagreement over other issues. Isaac Nelson was a commanding figure, although too unpopular to dominate. And there were no Cunninghams and Candlishs in Ireland to manage the debates and decisions in 1846 with the skill of the accomplished ecclesiastical politicians that they had become. The battle, in the meantime in late 1846, moved to London, where preparations were being made for an international ecumenical gathering of evangelical churches.

Chapter 9
Evangelicals and Abolitionists – Houses Divided

The Evangelical Alliance

1846 saw the birth of the Evangelical Alliance, a worldwide fellowship of Churches and individuals committed to biblical orthodoxy and seeking Christian evangelism throughout the world. Treated with suspicion by many in the Church of England and the Church of Scotland, it was a natural body with which the Free Church of Scotland would identify. Thomas Chalmers was by this time in poor health, but Robert Candlish was amongst its founders and William Cunningham amongst the twenty-five Free Church of Scotland delegates at its first Conference.[1]

Candlish had been part of a preliminary meeting of the Aggregate Committee of the Alliance in Birmingham, England, in March 1846. He moved the controversial resolution that perhaps reflected his own conflicting feelings on the subject of slavery:

> That while this Committee deem it unnecessary and inexpedient to enter into any question at present on the subject of slave-holding, or on the difficult circumstances in which Christian brethren may be placed in countries where the law of slavery prevails, they are of the opinion that invitations ought not to be sent to individuals who, whether by their own fault or otherwise, may be in the unhappy position of holding their fellow-men as slaves.

There was considerable confusion when it came to the seventy-strong delegation from America who came to the first conference of the Alliance in London, in August of that year. In July the provisional Committee agreed to communicate the proposed ban to all, but, as Sidney Morse from New York told the Conference, this was far too late for many American delegates who were on their way already. John Adger, coming from Syria where he was a missionary, warned Thomas Smyth that they might not be welcome. In the event it was doubtful if any who were slave-holders attended. The issue was not raised until the ninth day of the Conference when J. Howard Hinton, a Baptist minister from

London, and a veteran of the movement to abolish slavery in the British Empire, rose. Hinton obviously felt that the Alliance's witness against slavery had been weak, and he moved a simple addendum in the discussion over defining membership – a phrase that was to trigger several days of torturous debate and ecclesiastical politicking.

The Conference had before them a statement of objectives and membership of the Alliance to which Howard Hinton was to insert the words 'not being slave-holders'. Quietly, but firmly, he argued that since it had been agreed that slave-holders could not come to the Conference, it was impossible to admit them to the Alliance. He did not deny that a slave-holder could be a Christian, but said that many of the British members, including himself, who could not sit with a slave-holder at the Lord's Table, could hardly receive him as a fellow member of the Alliance. Although Hinton rejected the tactics of the Garrisonian abolitionists, he recoiled equally from the prospect of the Alliance seeming to 'prop up and bolster the system of American slavery'. 'I would be loath to divide the Alliance', he concluded, 'but in point of fact the Alliance is divided already'.

Hinton's amendment was seconded by Joshua Himes of the Advent Church in Boston, the 'witness' cited by Smyth against Douglass, 'for the purity of the Alliance'. He told the Conference that 'so called Christian slave-holders' were 'the chief bulwarks of slavery', for, he claimed, 'the better the man, the more sanctity and support he gives to the abomination'. After opposition statements from several Americans, the first southerner to speak, Thomas Smyth, got to his feet, giving three reasons against the introduction of the issue of slavery.

Smyth argued that it was not 'a matter of Christian obligation' to consider the subject – for him it was 'unnecessary'. Secondly, he said that it was 'inexpedient', since all of them were against slavery, but this would work against the universality of the Alliance, and even divide the British members. Finally he pointed out that slavery was founded on political institutions, and the Alliance had no business to be involved in politics. He continued by citing a leading British Biblical scholar of the previous century, Bishop Samuel Horsley, in declaring that the indictment of 'man-stealing' in scripture purely referred to the trade in slaves, and not to slavery itself.

'I feel that we are standing on ground that is trembling under our feet', said Dr Ralph Wardlaw. He brought the Alliance back to a recognition of the sin of slavery and argued that they could not legislate for the exceptional cases of humane slave-holders. He concluded:

I must say Mr. Chairman, that I do regret the institution of two Alliances as a far less evil in its own nature, and as less evil in the results which are likely to arise from it-than that of its appearing to the World, that this great Alliance (supposing it to be one) was giving its countenance or sanction, directly or indirectly, to that accursed thing, Slavery, – either in the United States, or in any other part of the World.

Wardlaw's fellow Congregationalist, William Urwick from Dublin, attempted a compromise motion, which declared slavery as 'iniquitous' and 'repugnant to the genius of the gospel', rejoiced in progress made to its abolition, but declined to prescribe any course of action to be pursued, and hoped that all members would commit themselves to the cause. Not surprisingly, Wardlaw and a number of others could not agree with this, and the whole issue was remitted to a large committee, which included Howard Hinton and the hitherto silent Isaac Nelson of Belfast.

After hours of discussion, the Committee recommended the withdrawal of the Hinton amendment and the adoption of a Resolution which Hinton himself moved:

That in respect to the necessity of personal holiness, the Alliance are of opinion that it is recognised in the Articles of the Basis – On the work of the Spirit; and, in reference to various social evils existing in countries within the circle of this Alliance, such as the profanation of the Lord's day, intemperance, duelling, and the sin of slavery, they commend these and similar evils to the consideration of the Branches, trusting that they will study to promote the general purity and the Christian honour of this Confederation by all proper means. And, in respect especially to the system of slavery and any other form of oppression in any country, the Alliance are unanimous in deploring them, as in many ways obstructing the progress of the Gospel; and express their confidence, that no Branch will admit to Membership slaveholders, who, by their own fault, continue in that position, retaining their fellow-men in slavery, from regard to their interests.

For many delegates this seemed to recover the position articulated by Birmingham, and although Howard Hinton admitted that it was 'less rigid' than he would have wished, both he and Ralph Wardlaw concurred with the committee. But immediately Isaac Nelson shifted the ground when he moved an amendment 'that whereas it is impossible for this conference to legislate for particular cases or exceptions, *no Slave-owner be admitted to any Branch of the Alliance*'. He argued that if a slave-holder claimed that his situation was 'not his fault', under that resolution he would be admitted to the Alliance. Nelson was seconded by James Stanfield, his colleague in the Belfast Anti-Slavery Society, but they were swimming against the tide.

Inevitably a backlash came from the Americans. John Adger spelt out the southerners' position. He wished to enter 'decided and solemn protest' at any action with regard to slavery, and pointed out that the Presbyterian Church in America did not see a man as a sinner simply because he was a slave-holder. Several northerners supported him, and there was considerable feeling that the issue should not have been raised. In the event Nelson's amendment fell, and the Committee's motion was carried with only six dissenting votes.

The dispute, however, was far from over. The Americans continued to express their unhappiness, and the sense of being singled out by the mention of slavery. It was a Dublin judge, Philip Crampton, who recognised the strength of feeling and moved that the second half of the Resolution should be left out. Howard Hinton claimed that this was a motion 'for rejecting the Anti-Slavery friends from this Conference'. Ralph Wardlaw said that he and Hinton had with reluctance agreed to the Resolution, and any watering down might lead him to leave the Alliance. William Smart from the United Secession Church in Linlithgow claimed that if the Resolution was modified, 'till the American members be satisfied', the Alliance would 'with few exceptions, lose the whole of the Scottish Dissenters'.

The recommendation of the Committee was unanimous. Judge Crampton's amendment should be discarded; the 'arrangements and organisation' of the Alliance should be deferred till the next Conference, and at present separate Alliances for Britain and America should be recognised. With relief, Howard Hinton seconded the motion to accept this, but Isaac Nelson was not satisfied. He proposed yet another amendment which he eventually withdrew, but it kept the radical abolitionist position before the Conference. He moved:

> That it is the incumbent duty of this meeting to express its desire and opinion, that no person claiming the right to hold property in man be received into any affiliated Branch of this *Alliance*; as the reception of Slave-holders will disparage the character of this *Alliance*, and cause many Christians in Great Britain and Ireland to withdraw from its connection, and be the fruitful source of dissension hereafter.

Many of the Americans were furious. Samuel Cox, a Presbyterian minister from New York, accused Nelson of 'insolence', a remark he was forced to withdraw, and Hinton as 'not quite so gracious as the grace of God should have made him to be'. Isaac Nelson continued to question the compromise, but the conference was weary of the many days of dispute over slavery, and the Resolution to defer and delay was accepted. It was a relief to them all, although somewhat ironic that almost at the close of the conference, they were addressed by the newly arrived Mollison Madison Clark, an African American from Washington who ministered to a slave congregation.

Mollison Clark chose his words carefully with fulsome praise for the Alliance, and claimed to represent not just seventeen thousand of the African Methodist Episcopal Church, but three million slaves, on whose behalf he expressed himself 'highly gratified' by the deliberations of the Alliance. Most of his speech was taken up by reading out impressive statistics from his denomination, rather than expanding on the issue of slavery. This diplomatic position led to the other Americans tumbling over themselves to shower Clark with compliments. Robert Baird and Cox described him as 'a blessed brother', and Stephen Olin thanked 'the Providence of God' for bringing him and declared him a 'witness to the sentiments of the American brethren'. Even Ralph Wardlaw joined in this joy, telling the conference that he had been 'all along missing a coloured countenance amongst us'.[2]

Douglass Returns to Scotland but Emancipationists Divide

Frederick Douglass returned to Scotland in September 1846, this time accompanied by William Lloyd Garrison. Their first meeting was in Paisley, the scene of his many enthusiastic supporters as well as considerable opposition. Douglass began by delivering a delayed attack on the Free Church position at the Assembly in May. 'I heard at the Free Church Assembly', he thundered:

> Speeches delivered by Duncan, Cunningham, and Candlish, and I never heard, in all my life, speeches better calculated to uphold and sustain that bloody system of wrong. [Cheers] I heard sentiments such as those from Dr Candlish – that Christians would be quite justified in sitting down with a slave-holder at a communion table- with men who have the right, by the laws of the land, to kill their slaves. That sentiment, as it dropped from the lips of Dr Candlish, was received by three

thousand people with shouts of applause.

The Biblical scholar John Duncan unsurprisingly came in for some heavy condemnation for his change of position from 'choking' if forced to eat with slave-holders, and his new distinction between 'slave-holders' and 'slave-havers' who were innocent inheritors of slaves. 'He has coined a new name', retorted Douglas':

> Oh! What delight flashed through the whole Assembly when the discovery was made. Were I a slave-holder? Candlish smiled, so did Cunningham, and all the younglings of the Free Church opened their mouths. I won't ask Dr Duncan what has changed his heart, but what has changed his stomach. He would dare to ridicule the only true antislavery man among them, who was Mr. Macbeth.

Douglass then moved to attack Cunningham's assertion that the law of the land in America made it impossible for people to avoid slave-holding. 'Let us suppose', he asked 'the law should make all domestics the concubines of their employers – that he would be bound to sustain the relation, would Dr Cunningham do it?' Douglass gave the obvious answer to that rhetorical question that he would 'not sustain the relationship, because he believes it to be wrong, and that it would not be sustained by the morality of the religious sentiment of Scotland for a moment'.

The contention that Christian slaveholders could not be blamed for observing the law was made by Chalmers, Cunningham and Candlish, but it was a bit of an Achilles heel for the Free Church argument. Although Douglass at times simply used invective – 'The Free Church is built up by robbery and wrong' – he was on solid ground when he returned to the theme of the Free Church going to America in the name of freedom, but avoiding any challenge to the enslavement of millions of Americans and to the laws which prevented slaves from reading the Bible. 'You might carry them (Bibles) to Hindostan and circulate them there, 'he said 'but you cannot circulate them amongst the slaveholders'.

Since the meeting was in Paisley, Frederick Douglass took the opportunity to score points from his old adversary John Macnaughton, of the town's High Kirk. To laughter he insisted on terming Macnaughton 'my brother', and detailed how the minister had 'poured out vials of wrath' on George Thompson, Henry C. Wright, and Douglass himself in Newcastle, where they were all speaking, but had been unwilling to meet them. Macnaughton's unwise earlier comment about Douglass as 'a poor miserable fugitive slave' and an 'ignorant one' drew a sharp response, when Douglass proclaimed to a cheering audience, 'I say such a man is not worthy to be called a Christian minister, when he can speak thus of brethren deprived of their privileges'.[3]

At two other meetings, in Edinburgh and Glasgow, Frederick Douglass concentrated on the Evangelical Alliance. James Robertson of the Scottish Anti-Slavery Society and the Quaker John Wigham argued at a meeting in Edinburgh that 'free negroes' in America viewed 'the conduct of the Free Church in a strong light'. Douglass cited Candlish's proposal to exclude slave-holders from the conference. He then detailed the composition of the American delegation in August, who all claimed that the Birmingham decision was not yet binding. With some justification, he showed how the Americans tried to get the issues of slavery made taboo at the Conference – 'They loved the Alliance, but they loved slavery far better'. With less than fairness, he described the result of Thomas Smyth's proposal for the committee to resort to prayer as, praying 'for some loophole for the slaveholder to be admitted into the Evangelical Alliance'.[4]

If Douglass's description of the delegates at the Alliance showing their prayers as 'blasphemy before God', with 'a keener sense of sheep stealing than of man stealing' was going too far, his frustration at what he saw as compromise over the issue was understandable. Part of that was caused by other denominations – the United Secession Church and the Relief Synod had recently declared that they would have no fellowship with any American churches, whilst slavery was tolerated by them. Another factor in his frustration was the perception that what he called 'the uncompromising advocates of emancipation' in Glasgow, had 'ceased to work with us'. At a meeting at the end of September in Glasgow's City Hall, Douglass specifically listed those who were not the 'eminent Doctors of Divinity'.

These were Dr David King, minister of Greyfriars United Presbyterian Church, Dr John Robson of Wellington Street Secession Church and the redoubtable Ralph Wardlaw. Wardlaw, for Douglass, had agreed to the 'abominable compromise' of the Alliance, and King and Robson had been silent. The tone here by Douglass was of sadness, but it soon turned to bitterness when he attacked two of his own countrymen, one white, and the other black. His old adversary Thomas Smyth was again blamed for offering hospitality to the Free Church delegation, and requesting the prayers of the delegates at the Evangelical Alliance, in order to get support for Southern slavery. 'He is the same Dr Smyth', said Douglass, 'who lives in the midst of slave-owners and slave-drivers, and never opens his mouth on slavery – the same Dr Smyth who is the unblushing advocate of slavery'.

The harshest condemnation, however, came for the cooperation with the Alliance by Mollison Madison Clark described as 'a recreant black man in this country'. Clark, for Douglass:

> Went into that Alliance and there denounced the only true friends of emancipation – the abolitionists. If he goes through this country, as I expect he will, for I expect that the Free Church of Scotland will employ him to go about and defend her, as he has the Judas Iscariot impudence to stand up in defence of her connection with the man stealers of America; and I trust he will be informed that I arraigned him here as a traitor to his race, and representing no portion of the black, or coloured population, in the United States.

In fact Clark never commented on the abolitionists in his speech. Douglass at the end of his Scottish tour showed signs of struggling to convince his audience, if not himself, of the success of his cause, and it led him to a number of misjudgements. 'Let not the *Warders, Witnesses,* or *Guardians* [three newspapers sympathetic to the Free Church] suppose', he said, 'that the cry raised against the Free Church and the Evangelical Alliance is to be but a nine days wonder', but perhaps he feared that it was so. After a eulogy on Garrison, he proclaimed his determination to keep 'the conduct of the Free Church before the people' and proclaim that in answer to questions on the Sabbath, church membership, or other questions, he would reply 'Send back the money'.[5] It was a much more stilted slogan by this time, and although the attendance was described as 'numerously' or 'poorly', according to the sympathies of different Glasgow newspapers, there was a sense of recognition that anti-slavery activity was weaker and less clear cut in Scotland. This reflected the splits amongst the abolitionists, which were to bedevil the cause even into the 1860s when America was plunged into civil war.

Scotland in the 1840s was beginning to reflect the divisions in the Anti-Slavery Movement in America. Lewis Tappan, the New York businessman who had written to the Free Church delegation in 1844, had co-founded, with William Lloyd Garrison, the pioneer American Anti-Slavery Society in the 1830s, but in 1840 he parted company with him over the issues of Women's Suffrage and Feminism. Tappen and his brother then founded the American and Foreign Anti-Slavery Society. The Society should have commended itself to the Free Church, since it upheld the literal truth of Scripture and believed that abolitionism would be achieved by appeals to moral persuasion rather than political action. The philosophy and tactics of Tappan's organisation seemed very much to fit the position taken by the leadership of the Free Church. That might have been so in other circumstances, but the Free Church's acceptance of Southern money and the goodwill of Southern churches, boxed them in and made even the demands of the most modest abolitionists, a bridge too far.[6]

Tappan and his associates were never able to build an effective anti-slavery movement. The Garrisonians, though to some extent a Bostonian movement, was also a national one through *The Liberator*. As has been seen, they embraced a wide range of issues and different styles of speakers. At this point Frederick Douglass was wholeheartedly supported by Garrison but there were to be quarrels between them later on, not least because Douglass supported recruitment of African Americans for the Union side in the Civil War, whilst Garrison had no time either for war or the defence of the American Constitution.

The successor body to the British Anti-Slavery Society of the 1830s was the British and Foreign Anti-Slavery Society founded in 1839 and led mainly by Quakers from England. It rejected Garrisonian tactics and philosophy, and allied with Tappan's American and Foreign Anti-Slavery Society. Douglass, in keeping with his policy of cooperation with all abolitionist bodies, dined with the Society's founder Joseph Sturge in Birmingham in December 1845 and several months later addressed Sturge's movement, something which did not please Garrison.

This split was reflected in the various Scottish societies. The Edinburgh and Glasgow Emancipation Societies had been founded in 1833 to replace the old ones which had campaigned against slavery in the British Empire. After the 1841 American split, they began to take different paths, and in one significant way divided an abolitionist dynasty. Eliza Wigham, who accompanied Douglass to carve out the slogan on the Edinburgh Crags, as Secretary of the Edinburgh Ladies Emancipation Society gave unqualified support to Garrison's cause, and organised collections of materials for the Boston Bazaar, a great anti-slavery fundraiser there. At the same time her father was a key figure in the more conservative and male Edinburgh Emancipation Society. His second wife Jane was not only a key figure in the ladies society, but supported her brother William Smeal of the Glasgow Emancipation Society, who not only remained fiercely loyal to Garrison throughout the 1840s, but hosted

Frederick Douglass and gave uncritical support to Henry C. Wright. The Glasgow Emancipationists, who lost the enthusiasm of some of their key supporters, such as Ralph Wardlaw, during this period, were bankrupted by the 'Send Back the Money' Campaign, and only re-emerged as an effective body in 1851.

The short-lived Scottish Anti-Slavery Society, under James Robertson, was founded to replace the Edinburgh body and unify anti-slavery activity in Scotland. It made an attempt to engage both Smyth and his Free Church friends, in debate with the abolitionists. Yet it foundered, partly because of the strength of the Glasgow Society, whose members were in no mood to compromise their support for Garrison, or cede their control to the capital. Although Douglass and Thompson were prepared to support both bodies, the Scottish abolitionists reflected all too clearly the disunity that was affecting Americans committed to the abolition of slavery. All this did not help those few within the Free Church of Scotland, who had a passion for the same cause.

The Free Church Anti-Slavery Society – a late entry on the scene

In early May 1846, frustration from a number of the Free Churchmen over the now successful attempts to silence any dissident voices, led to the formation of The Free Church Anti-Slavery Society. The society did not really start until the late summer when its rules and objectives were adopted. The latter were defined as seeking to 'impress on the public mind' through the means of lectures, meetings, and what were described as 'circulation of authentic documents'. Their key points were defined as:

1. The sin and danger of admitting Slave-holders to the Communion of Christian Churches.
2. The duty of relinquishing Christian Fellowship with Slave-holding Churches.
3. The necessity of aiding generally the cause of the Immediate Emancipation of the Slave.

The usual arrangements for office bearers were spelt out, the subscription set at one shilling annually, and membership restricted to 'members' or 'adherents' of the Free Church with a bracketed statement of both 'Male and Female'. The publication of the Laws was made by Charles Ziegler, printer and bookseller in South Bridge, Edinburgh, and an enthusiastic abolitionist. Although the Society held meetings these were not extensively covered in the press, its main activity was to sponsor and distribute pamphlets over 1847 and 1848

The isolation of James Macbeth in the 1846 General Assembly at the same time that Douglass, Garrison, and Thompson were drawing huge appreciative audiences, indicated the rift between the Free Church and so many other churchmen in Scotland. *The Witness* was scathing about the formation of this new Society, perhaps reflecting the fear of the damage to relationships with America which it posed. The Committee included a number of well known churchmen including Isaac Nelson, but only two were ministers of the Free Church – Michael Willis, the first President, and James Macbeth one of the two Vice-Presidents.

The Society set out its policy in a pamphlet addressed to 'the Office-Bearers and Members of the Free Church of Scotland' shortly before the 1847 General Assembly.

It has been suggested that this was the work of James Macbeth, and certainly it bears the hallmarks of his style.[7] Setting out the policy of the Society by protesting the Society's loyalty to the Free Church, the author then moved to challenge specific policies included in the remonstrance and in the Assembly speeches. The idea that the Free Church was 'brought, by the providence of God, into her present connection with the American churches' had, for him, been used to justify the status quo. It was, however, pointed out that fellowship with 'slave-holding churches' had involved a conscious choice by the Free Church. God should not be held responsible. Then there was a challenge to the distinction between 'slave-holding' and 'slave-having' made by John Duncan. 'Dr Duncan' may speak, said the writer, of 'wicked laws by which a slave-holder is forbidden to emancipate his slave' but 'whoever deprives another of liberty is a man-stealer in the eyes of God . . . and all such distinctions are spiders webs to screen the guilty man from the light of truth and the thunderbolts of justice'.

The pamphlet then attacked, with some scorn, the idea that some men could not help being slave-holders and that to resist a situation in which they have been placed by God might itself be sinful. In tones reminiscent of a Douglass speech, the writer pointed out that there may be people who 'cannot help' lying or stealing but this merely aggravated the sin, since they have become impervious to any moral restraints. He continued by quoting Candlish's assertion that emancipation might be 'a sin against the slave and against God', and challenged him to demonstrate what divine precepts this would violate, and what burden would be laid on a person in bondage.

The argument moved to take up the question of whether Jesus and his apostles admitted slave-holders into the church. Without pointing out the obvious fact that there was no church in the time of Jesus, the writer asserted strongly that the apostles did not countenance it. He noted that in the 1846 Assembly when James Macbeth had supported this position, John Duncan had declared that he would 'be ashamed' to have used Macbeth's arguments. Robert Cunningham too had spoken slightingly of Macbeth's ideas, declaring that he 'thought them without foundation', and 'did not expect to hear them openly and broadly brought up in the face of the General Assembly of the Free Church of Scotland'. This, the writer considered somewhat ungracious, 'for all his high intellectual and moral worth' towards a man who 'stood alone in the Assembly'. He added that it might well startle Drs Candlish and Cunningham to find themselves 'appealing to the same [biblical] passages which were urged against the work of Clarkson, Wilberforce, and Dr Andrew Thomson'.[8]

Andrew Thomson's name was raised again later, but not before the writer made a long and not entirely convincing argument about Philemon and Onesimus. Instead of echoing James Macbeth's position that the Greek word *doulos* meant servant, rather than slave, the writer concentrated on Paul's statement of Onesimus being 'a brother beloved, in the flesh and in the Lord' and took it to mean that there was a filial relationship with Philemon. Even if that strange interpretation had been literally true, it was all too clear at this time that any 'octoroon' with seven-eighths white blood in America was not protected from the full horrors of enslavement.

Towards the end of the pamphlet the writer made a full scale attack on the way in which the leadership of the Free Church had used the memory of Andrew Thomson to support their criticism of the abolitionists. 'The sentiments advanced by Dr Candlish' said the writer:

Are totally opposed to those held by Dr Thomson on the subject of slavery. Ask Dr Thomson if it is the duty of everyone to emancipate his slaves' and that mighty man replies, 'it is the duty of every person who has a slave to emancipate him immediately.' Ask Dr Thomson of the awful consequences that would result if the American church were to insist on immediate emancipation and he answers 'give me the hurricane, rather than the pestilence.'[9] Ask Dr Thomson what he thinks of the argument adduced from scripture, to prove, and he replies with his usual frankness – 'the public mind has been sickened and disgusted, by the miserable sophistry and scriptural dogmas which certain modern divines have been sporting'.

Chapter 10
The Last Battles and Hunting 'the brave Macbeth'

We entreat you not to neglect this opportunity of advancing the cause of the slave, for we humbly believe, that, if the Free Church would at once renounce the position which she now occupies, slavery would receive a blow from which it would never recover.

Leaflet/Letter from Eliza Wigham, *Edinburgh Ladies Emancipation Society*, 4 March 1847

The 1847 General Assembly

Although the resulting impact of the Free Church Anti-Slavery Society was in some respects to harden support around the leadership of the Free Church, it also seemed to disturb some commissioners at the 1847 Assembly enough to raise questions. Out in the country there were a number of petitions that found their way to the Assembly managers. One was from the Deacons Court of St. Bernard's Free Church in Edinburgh, and it went straight to the point in making 'a plain and full declaration':

1st Of the principle that every man is entitled to the enjoyment of freedom as an inalienable right.

2nd That the Free Church of Scotland cannot hold fellowship with Churches countenancing slaveholding, or failing to use proper efforts for its abolition.

3rd That in respect to the American Presbyterian Churches, the Free Church address to them a solemn remonstrance, testifying against the great sin they have committed in taking into communion as members, many who hold their fellow creatures in slavery; and urging them to carry out more faithfully, according to the Word of God, that discipline which is indispensably requisite to preserve purity and good order in any church; and warning them, that until this be done, the Free Church cannot hold communion with them as brothers of the Church of Christ.

This, if carried in the Assembly, would have gone further than the Irish. Another petition from members, deacons and elders of Prestonpans Free Church fell somewhat short of that. It asked the Assembly to declare again its conviction that everyone was entitled to freedom. The petitioners also asked for a declaration that they could not hold communion with churches that were slave-holding or did not use 'proper measures' for the abolition of slavery. They wanted to disclaim any association with the Free Church Anti-Slavery Society or any group of abolitionists and, perhaps crucially, they declared their belief that this was consistent with the position of the Free Church in whose General Assembly decisions they had utmost confidence.[1]

William Cunningham dismissed the first petition on the grounds that while individuals could petition the Assembly, Deacons Courts could not. This was challenged by Dr Patrick Clason, one of the Assembly Clerks, but Cunningham simply said that the procedure would be remitted to a later decision. Robert Candlish gave a fulsome reply to the second petition, rather patronisingly praising it as 'very courteous, temperate, firm and respectful' and rejoicing in the somewhat doubtful assertion that there was no difference of opinion between the views and principles held by the petitioners of Prestonpans and himself. He then told the Assembly that since nothing had been received from the American churches in response to the Free Church's last communication, then the Committee would not recommend any further action to the Assembly. Decision, if not discussion, was virtually dead at this stage.

Robert Candlish continued by citing a petition signed by 1871 elders, deacons, members and adherents of the Free Church. An analysis of this showed that the signatories came from Ayrshire, Glasgow, Lanarkshire and East Lothian. It was, he thought, a tribute to the unanimity of the Church on this matter that the petition had fewer than two thousand signatures over such a wide geographical area. Several petitions had arrived from various bodies and individuals but had been deemed invalid. He wanted to inform the Assembly the reason for this variety and held up a circular which had come into his hands in April. It was dated 'Edinburgh 4 March 1847'. It began by reminding the reader of the Free Church of Scotland's 'cherishing religious communion with the slaveholders of America'. The price of this was the £3,000 contributed by the slave-holders of the South. Entreaties on this subject have so far been rejected, said the writer, who advised all 'as members of the one universal church' to plead with these brethren in error to acknowledge their fault.

Every anti-slavery Society and congregation or 'associated body of professing Christians' were urged to send remonstrances to the Free Church General Assembly directed to the Moderator before 20 May 1847. The letter concluded:

> We entreat you not to neglect this opportunity of advancing the cause of the slave, for we humbly believe, that, if the Free Church would at once renounce the position which she now occupies, slavery would receive a blow from which it would never recover. We would be glad to know your sentiments on these suggestions and whether we may depend on your co-operation at this important juncture. We are, dear friends, yours, for the cause of the slave (signed on behalf of the Committee of the Edinburgh Ladies Emancipation Society) ELIZA WIGHAM, Secretary.

Candlish read this letter out with suitable pauses and frequent brief comments. The reading was punctuated with laughter in the Assembly. Despite mocking it and pointing out that it had only produced between half-a-dozen and a dozen results, and effectively killed any effect the letter might have had, he nonetheless felt it necessary to go on the offensive once more. 'The real friends of the slave' he asserted, were not prepared to mix it up 'with questions of ecclesiastic discipline ... far less to damage the cause they love, by making it the occasion, or the pretence, for an attack on any religious body'.

He then questioned whether anyone wanted to 'undo' what had been done – the sending of the delegation to American and the reception of what he repeatedly called 'tokens of sympathy and love' from the American churches. Even in the Presbytery of Glasgow, he said, 'the brethren who support the views which some regard as extreme, – namely Dr Willis and Mr Macbeth' did not advocate further discussion of the delegation. Candlish then went on to criticise the letter sent to America from the Presbyterian Church in Ireland. It showed, he felt, a keenness to indicate that they were 'more decidedly' against slavery than the Free Church, without taking any position that would separate themselves from the Free Church stance. He did, however, say that there was much in the American reply that 'pained and grieved' him and he felt that the judgement of the American churches had been 'warped' by 'the influences of living in the midst of that accursed system, the abominations of American slavery'.

Once more Cunningham told the Assembly that he did not need to enter at length on the subject, and once more he proceeded to do. He reaffirmed the reasons for waiting until the next American response came before considering action. He further reaffirmed that the church was strongly against 'the sinful nature, the degrading character, the injurious character of slavery', and he reaffirmed that the real difference between the Free Church and the abolitionists was not how much they hated slavery but the impolity of denying communion to slave-owners, something for which again he denied any scriptural warrant.

Cunningham was not convinced that a church that admitted slaveholders was guilty of 'heresy', a charge that at various points in history had warranted a break in fellowship. In what was perhaps a remark aimed at the Church of Scotland he said that he believed the communion-roll of the American Presbyterian Church to be 'purer' than that of 'the Presbyterians of this country' with 'a larger portion of converted men' and he felt that they could not be blamed for all the evils of society.

Finally Cunningham had strong words for what he called 'the agitation which has been got up on this subject . . . with the desire of injuring the Free Church'. Quoting the renowned pioneer missionary, Dr Alexander Duff of India, he said that such agitation was 'an ingenious device of Satan to injure the church'. Incredibly he spoke of 'the Garrisons, the Wrights, the Buffens, the George Thompsons and the Douglasses' in whom he was sure 'with that class of persons, the character which they exhibited, the spirit which they manifested' he thought that 'Satan entirely outwitted himself'. To laughter and cheers from the Assembly he continued to claim that all of these abolitionists 'disgusted the Christian people of this land' and he concluded by expressing the belief (correctly as it turned out) that the Free Church Anti-Slavery Society would not last long. He predicted that 'every man of good principle, good sense, and good feeling, who has any professed regards for Christian liberty, will soon abandon altogether any connection with it'.

Cunningham sat down to great applause but his words in different circumstances might have led to a libel suit. They certainly killed any chance of further debate. One speaker suggested that the remonstrance to America should be strong, Dr James Grierson of Errol, while proclaiming his agreement with everything that was said, ended his speech by suggesting that the Free Church should be prepared to give five times the £3,000 in order to carry forward the glorious cause of emancipation'. He received applause but Sheriff Spiers at length told the Assembly that nothing could be said or done until a reply had been received from the Americans. For the first

time the Assembly heard the text of the response sent to America
after the 1846 Assembly.

Sheriff Spiers claimed that it showed how unjust a judgement on
the Free Church Eliza Wigham's circular had been, but it's apologetic
tone of 'not dicatating' to the Americans and mild condemnation
of those who choose the permits of the law over against the divine
duty on slavery, were hardly likely to convince abolitionists within
or outside the Free Church that they were all united on the issue.
Once again Cunningham rose and repeated that they were under no
obligation to repeat their condemnation of slavery and Candlish said
that he hoped 'the House would not be hurried into any premature
step in this matter'. It wasn't.

Strictures, Pamphlets, and another Assembly

The frustration of the Free Church Anti-Slavery Society in the face
of the attacks on abolitionism and the refusal to go beyond polite
questions to the American churches was reflected in another long
address entitled *Strictures on the Proceedings of the Last General
Assembly*. The author of this was believed to be Dr Michael Willis,
now President of the Free Church Anti-Slavery Society.[2] Later that
year he was to accept a call to be Professor of Theology in the new
theological college in Toronto, Canada. It was as if this all but last
stand of the Society had abandoned all attempts at conciliation
with the Free Church leadership and resorted to a more hectoring
and complaining mode. There was an initial attack on *The Witness*
and the other press sympathetic to the Free Church for alleged
misrepresentation of Isaac Nelson. Willis claimed that the subject of
slavery had been closed to the columns of *The Witness* whilst the
views of an American owner of a newspaper which circulated in
the South as well as the North were given free rein. Another and
stronger point was made about petitions that were never heard in
the General Assembly, including one from the Society which was
'condemned without a hearing'.

Although that was open to question, there was more substance in
the complaint against Cunningham, who had intemperately accused
Garrison, Buffen, Thompson and Douglass of doing the work of
Satan. Willis made the obvious response that communion with
slave-holders was more likely to give pleasure to the devil, that Jesus
himself was accused of having a devil, and that 'Papists' claimed
that Martin Luther had a 'cloven foot'. A number of pages were then
taken in a response to what the Society saw as Cunningham's inability

Eliza and Jane Wigham and Mary Estlin (a Bristol abolitionist)

to hold together the sinfulness of slavery and the circumstances in which men may hold others in slavery without sinning. 'During the controversy' says the author:

Dr Cunningham has found one position after another untenable, at last he is shut up in a corner where further retreat is impossible: like the monarch of the waters when driven before the storm, till he is stranded in a narrow creek, where he may be harpooned with safety, by the most timid and

unskilled landsman. Finding slavery incapable of defence on
natural principles, or on any of those political principles which
lie at the foundation of all society, whether civil or religious,
he had retired into the citadel of revelation, as if Christianity
were the stronghold of his cause, as if the Bible, among other
ends, had been given by inspiration, in order to protect the
character of Slave-holders, by securing their admission into
the Church, when there was no place of refuge left for them
on earth – just as the temple of the Lord was still a sanctuary
for those malefactors, who, everywhere else, would have been
unsafe.

It was of course wildly optimistic to portray Southern slave-owners
at this stage as fugitives seeking refuge in the Church. It was equally
unrealistic to portray Cunningham stranded within society, let
alone within the Free Church. There was a milder but perhaps more
effective 'stricture' on Candlish. The pamphlet quoted his expressed
opinion on March 1844, when, in response to the death sentence on
the first John Brown he had argued that the Churches should 'wash
their hands' of others who 'tolerate the sin of slavery by admitting
slave-holders to communion'. [3] Naturally the Society discerned
a volte-face by the Assembly of 1845 and his attitude in 1846 it
regarded as 'a natural progress of error'.

Candlish seemed has been somewhat driven into a corner
himself. He was challenged by the address to espouse 'the doctrine
of immediate emancipation' as propounded so eloquently by Dr
Andrew Thomson and with which he seemed to agree when he told
the 1847 Assembly, 'I am not aware that anyone in this house for
a moment calls into question that the immediate emancipation of
the slave is a duty'. Having discovered what the Society deemed
to be Candlish's return to the abolitionist fold, they said that they
felt 'assured' that 'it is merely the first fruits of a coming harvest of
concessions'.[4]

It was a forlorn hope. Less than forty-eight hours after the
Assembly debate on slavery in May 1847 the death of Dr Thomas
Chalmers was announced. This not only overshadowed the whole
Assembly (business was suspended for a day) but occupied the
attention of the Free Church leadership for the immediate future.
At the same time and perhaps because American slavery had taken
a back seat in the priorities of the management of the Free Church,
its Anti-Slavery Society was prolific in the production of pamphlets
under their auspices.

The Society's Vice President, James Macbeth, in one of his

pamphlets, claimed that there was no evidence to show that the petitions which flooded into the 1847 Assembly were from those who were enemies of the Free Church and bent on its destruction. That was certainly true, but as Duncan Rice has pointed out, the four pamphlets circulated by the Free Church Anti-Slavery Society were all written by ministers of other churches. George Gilfillan, the Dundee Congregationalist who had hosted Frederick Douglass, was one. The second writer, George Jeffrey, United Secessionist Minister in Glasgow's London Road, had robustly attacked American slavery, when chairing a meeting addressed by Douglass and Buffen. The third, Isaac Nelson, was of course the man who had influenced the Irish Presbyterians on slavery and helped to found the Free Church Anti-Slavery Society. The fourth was David Young, United Secession Minister of Perth North Church. All were resolute in their opposition to the Free Church's position on slavery. But it is too simplistic to characterise them all, as Rice did, with general 'grievances against the Free Church'. Nelson at least, and to some extent Gilfillan, had as much of a genuine love and admiration for the Free Church's position on church polity as they had disappointment at its position on slavery.

George Jeffrey was the son-in-law of John Ritchie. Taking his cue from Frederick Douglass, in his pamphlet he gave a strong account of American slavery and an equally strong conviction that the American churches were deeply involved in its fabric. Isaac Nelson instanced George Thompson having to flee from America in 'doing his duty' and quoted Rev. Thomas Witherspoon from Alabama declaring, 'I draw my warrant from the scriptures of the Old and New Testament to hold the slave in bondage. The principle of holding the heathen in bondage is recognised by God'.

David Young's argument was that there must be a united and Christianised movement to 'testify and assist the abolitionists'. This could only happen, for him, if scripture and humanity are taken seriously over the sin of slavery. George Gilfillan, another veteran campaigner against British colonial slavery in the 1830s, talked of the 'stain' on a nation that it brought to nations. His analysis was that the Free Church had not intended to fraternise with slave-owners but, he maintained, 'the deputation committed a blunder, and that blunder defended, persisted in, defended by such arguments, persisted in such a spirit, became a crime'.[5]

The problem was that by mid 1847 the stable door had been effectively shut to the subject of slavery by the managers of the Free Church. If earlier communications between the abolitionists inside and outside the church and its leadership had assumed a dialogue of the deaf, by this time one side had in fact left the room. In the report of the 1848 Assembly, American slavery does not get a mention. In a few lines it is stated that towards the end of the Assembly, the Report of the Committee on Relations with the American Churches was given and approved, and that the Assembly approved a draft of an answer to the letter from the Presbyterian Church of America.[6] From then on the matter died as far as the Free Church was concerned. But it still had issues to conclude with one of the most doughty opponents of its policy on slavery.

The pamphlets of James Macbeth

Rev. James Macbeth was characterised by Frederick Douglass in Paisley in September 1846 as 'the only true anti-slavery man among them'. George Gilfillan was even more enthusiastic. 'Honour to that faithful Abdiel of the cause', he wrote:

> The brave Macbeth of Glasgow, who dared, amidst insulting inattention from the 'Sultan' of the party, and open derision from its underlings, to deliver his soul at the last General Assembly. It was no matter that the great ones read newspapers and the small ones chattered jokes, as his speech proceeded he spoke to a wider audience than the Canonmills Hall could contain. He spoke to the heart, principle and conscience of Scotland, and he did not speak in vain.[7]

In 1846 Macbeth had a pamphlet printed entitled *No Fellowship with Slave-holders*. It was, as he termed it, 'A calm review' of the 1846 debate in the Assembly and addressed 'respectfully to the Assembly of 1847, and to Members and Kirk Sessions' of the Free Church. Some months later he wrote a very different pamphlet entitled *The Church and the Slaveholder or Light and Darkness*. This explored biblical and theological themes, and reflected on the position taken on slavery by other Churches and by Christian luminaries. It was, again 'respectfully' addressed to the 'members of the approaching Assembly of the Free Church of Scotland, and to the Churches generally'.[8]

'I desire to write nothing', said James Macbeth, 'inconsistent with the spirit of brotherhood'. He denied that his was 'an extreme opinion' – it was the defence of slavery that merited that accusation. When the Synod of the Reformed Presbyterian Church in July determined to deny fellowship to slave-holders – was this, he asked, an extreme position? Macbeth listed the numerous churches in Scotland and England who adopted this position, and observed that Dr Cunningham, who claimed to speak for Christendom, needed to take into account the many Christian bodies that parted company with him. In response to Cunningham's attack on him for inconsistency, Macbeth argued the inconsistency of the Free Church refusing a relationship with the Church of Scotland, never inviting their ministers to preach, or be guests at the Assembly, but wanting a 'union of intercourse' with a church that was 'fifty times as Erastian'. It was, he claimed, the duty of the Church to remonstrate with the state on evil, but 'there is an historic fact that this American church has never once petitioned Congress against slavery'.[9]

He then turned to the disputed question of slavery being approved in the New Testament, and slave-owners admitted to the Lord's Supper in the early church. Much ink was spilt in challenging the interpretation of the Greek words *kurios* and *doulos* as slave-holder and slave. Whilst the Free Church leaders claimed that Paul accepted slavery in his treatment of Onesimus, Macbeth replied that 'Paul's letter bore in its bosom the liberty of Onesimus'. In response to Cunningham's assertion that 'it is clear and unquestionable in the New Testament that the apostles admitted slave-owners to the Lord's Table and recognised them as Christians', he responded that this was guesswork, of which there was no proof at all.

In the light of Dr Duncan's attempt at the 1846 Assembly to make the distinction between slave-holding and slave-having Macbeth retorted: 'There is as good a distinction between concubine-holding and concubine-having. Let no man dream that this hot-house subtlety will live in the open air of Scotland'. He challenged those who made these distinctions to ask the slaves to judge the difference. Macbeth denied that he and the Free Church Anti-Slavery Society ever argued for a total abandonment of contacts with the American church. 'We must keep friendly intercourse' he wrote ' but we must exclude from pulpit, courts and communion table this church until it repent and arouse itself'.[10]

The Church and the Slaveholder or Light and Darkness was a wide discourse by James Macbeth which avoided direct responses to the position of other individuals. The pamphlet is threaded throughout with the idea that 'every man [women didn't get a mention] is born free' and has 'inherent rights'. In case this might be thought to be too secular (Macbeth quoted the Virginia Bill of Rights on freedom, an irony in a slave state) John Wesley was cited, as was the Divine gift of rights. A magistrate, argued Macbeth, obtained his power and authority to punish and imprison from God, but a slave-holder had no such authority. There was, for him, no 'divine warrant for slavery' any more than there was 'a divine warrant for extermination' except for specific situations in the Bible.

A great deal of the pamphlet was devoted to biblical arguments and examples of the horrors of slavery. He mentioned that George Lewis of Dundee had noted that, whilst slavery was a banned topic at the 1844 Assembly, in 1794 American Presbyterians condemned slavery at the same gathering. This was not surprising, said Macbeth, when Professor Hodge of Princeton Seminary had declared 'the assumption that slave-holding is, in itself, a crime, is not only an error but it is fraught with evil consequences'. Many liberal Presbyterian congregations, claimed Macbeth, exclude slave-holders, and should be supported in this.

James Macbeth combined in his writing some wide elements of charity, whilst being uncompromising in holding to his convictions. He wished to see friendly and loving communication with American Presbyterian brothers, but to refuse any collusion with their situation. That was what made him a moral threat to those who wished to sweep the issue under the carpet. In no way did he want to imply, he declared, that all ministers in the slave states were 'unconverted men' and he went on to point out that John Newton continued to run a slave ship after his conversion. However, he also made the point that as with King David, Newton later repented every day of his involvement and encouraged William Wilberforce to rid the world of the 'accursed trade'.

Macbeth requested that none of his readers should see the issue as 'paltry'. The final decision of the Free Church would, for him, demonstrate whether its members loathed the American system of turning men into what John Wesley described as 'human cattle', and would 'venerate, where they are found, whether on the shores of Sutherland and on the moor of Canonbie, but across the Atlantic, the heaven erected and awful nature of man'.[11]

Serious charges against the minister of Lauriston

In March 1848 the Free Church Presbytery of Glasgow held a special meeting, at the request of James Macbeth, to deal with 'certain charges brought against him, to the effect that he had endeavoured to induce different individuals to commit adultery'.

After hearing from Macbeth, Presbytery set up a Committee of six ministers and one elder to investigate. By June they laid on the table evidence of witnesses and took legal advice from the Procurator, the church's legal adviser. Next month the procedure took a new turn since it was revealed that James Macbeth had raised a civil action against his accusers. In the meantime the Committee had concluded that there were 'serious matters for investigation' and new accusations had recently been made.

The Presbytery agreed to proceed with a libel.[12] This was prepared and served on James Macbeth, as reported to Presbytery on 8 November 1848.

He was accused of 'lasciviousness' and 'lewd approaches to women'. It was alleged that in June (or possibly in May or July) 1847, when his wife was away on the coast with the children and he was alone in the manse in Govan, he attempted 'to use improper liberties with a person named Grace Munro'. Grace was a servant of his neighbour who had been sent to help him in the house. When she was making up his bed, Macbeth was alleged to have pushed her against it, 'clapped her upon the shoulders' and offered her a shilling to sleep with him. The second charge was that in May 1846 (or April or June) on the day of his wife's confinement he enticed a servant, Catherine Somerville, to the bedroom 'for lewd and improper purposes' evidenced by the time he took to answer a knock on the door by another servant and by Catherine's emergence with 'her hair in a state of disorder'. The third charge was that when living in Kingston, Glasgow he had approached the bed of Martha Purdie, a married servant, ostensibly in order to place one of his infant children with her. He was alleged 'to have used immodest liberties with her person' and addressed her 'in filthy and obscene words'. The same scene was alleged to be enacted in his house in Govan.

Having instituted the proceedings against James Macbeth, the Presbytery was surprised and none too pleased to receive, that same night, details of a meeting of Macbeth's congregation of Laurieston Free Church which had resolved to send several resolutions to the Presbytery. The first of these informed the court of their sympathy for their minister 'in his present trying circumstances' and expressed the hope that he would be 'supported and strengthened'. The congregation, 'notwithstanding evil reports', declared their 'unanimous and unabated confidence in him as their spiritual teacher', commended all the benefits his ministry had brought them, and 'deeply regretted' that he had intimated his wish to be relieved of the pastoral charge. They requested that if it was 'consistent with the path of duty', he might 'continue to dispense the ordinances of

religion' among them. Every Monday members agreed to meet for
prayer in the church during his case.

The Presbytery, through clenched teeth, expressed satisfaction
for the congregation's confidence in, and support for, the minister,
but severely censured the office bearers for allowing or encouraging
such an action while Presbytery was deliberating on the matter.
They described the Kirk Session as 'ignorant', possibly in the
Glasgow sense of behaving inappropriately. By the spring of 1849
relationships deteriorated between Laurieston and the Presbytery,
when the elders understandably refused to insert Presbytery's
comments in the minute book of the Session. The following month
seven elders resigned in protest, and it took all the heavy weight of
the ecclesiastical lawmakers to browbeat the remaining elders into
submission to the higher court.

In the meantime the Presbytery decided that at their meeting on
29 March 1849 that James Macbeth was guilty of the first two charges
and that the third was 'not proven', a judgement uniquely open to
Scottish civil and eccelesiastical law. Macbeth appealed to the higher
court of the Synod of Glasgow and Ayr against these judgements
and on ten other counts where he felt the Presbytery had refused
him the right to examine witnesses or to hear the evidence of other
witnesses.[13]

The process continued from 27 April to 2 May. The Synod
overturned the first two of the Presbytery's judgements, finding by
large majorities James Macbeth not guilty on the first two counts,
but confirming the 'not proven' verdict on the third, with some
reservations about part of the charge. At one point dissent was
entered by John Macnaughton of Paisley, the protagonist with
Douglass, who may not have agreed with Macbeth on the slavery
issue, but clearly felt that Synod was too unfair. Neither side was
entirely satisfied, and both appealed to the General Assembly of
1849. Macbeth asked that the proceedings should be held in open
court, but William Cunningham successfully moved that press and
public be excluded. After a number of motions the Assembly upheld
the Synod's verdict of 'not proven' by the narrow margin of 109
votes to 103.

Macbeth had kept a dignified silence, whilst accepting a voluntary
suspension from his ministry in Laurieston. He even offered to pay
some of the costs of printing the materials of the case which was to go
back before the General Assembly of 1850. Clearly he was exhausted
by the whole business. He waived his right to insist that the Synod
instruct the Presbytery to implement its verdict regarding the first

two charges. Two office bearers had been found to support some of the accusations, for even in the most supportive congregations there are always those with grievances against the minister. On 23 May 1850, just before the General Assembly could deal further with the case, James Macbeth wrote to the Presbytery demitting (resigning) his charge and his status as a Free Church minister. He left shortly afterwards for Canada, where he completed the remainder of his ministry. Rather ridiculously, and despite a further letter from his ship, the Presbytery of Glasgow went with the case to the 1850 Assembly, which instructed them to proceed in the case 'according to the laws of the Church' and authorised the Commission of Assembly to 'pronounce final sentence in the case'. Even more ridiculously, the Presbytery held a meeting with the Laurieston office bearers to determine what could be done about 'a fugitive from discipline'.[14] Another stable door was about to be shut, but the horse had long since fled.

It was never conclusively proved that James Macbeth had been guilty of such behaviour, but he probably did himself no favours by neither admitting nor denying the charges. However, the support from the congregation in an era and a denomination where sexual improprieties were liable to call fire down on any minister, was extraordinary, to say the least. Conspiracy theories are often just that. However, it is hard to see as coincidence the fact that the most lone and isolated thorn in the flesh of the Free Church establishment in the embarrassing subject of slavery in 1846 and 1847, was the sole subject of accusations the following year that would lead to his exile from Scotland and the ministry of the Free Church. That connection was explicitly made by an anonymous author of a broadsheet circulated in Glasgow in 1849.[15] Whether by deliberate volition or not, at last the Free Church of Scotland would be free of an uncompromising opponent of fellowship with slave-owners.

Chapter 11
A Passing Storm in a Teacup
or the Shape of Things to Come?

*The public mind will be roused and the public indignation will cry
out – against the gross inconsistency of men calling themselves free,
patronising and encouraging slavery.*
Letter from 'Spectator' to *The Witness*, 2 May 1846

Unity and Division

Robert Burns once wrote 'facts are chiels that winna ding, and canna
be confounded'.[1] Facts there were in assessing this curious episode in
Scottish Church History. The Free Church Anti-Slavery Society soon
disappeared, and the most powerful abolitionist group in Scotland,
the Glasgow Emancipation Society, was bankrupted by the campaign
and did not re-emerge for a year or two. By 1850 the Free Church's
most resolute anti-slavery men – James Macbeth, Robert Burns, and
Michael Willis were all in Canada, Willis being a founding President
of the Canadian Anti-Slavery Society. With the death of Dr. Thomas
Chalmers, Drs Candlish and Cunningham extended their effective
control over the Free Church General Assembly, and their power
was in no way weakened by the 'Send Back the Money' Campaign.
Unsurprisingly, not a penny of the money was returned, nor was
there any break in fellowship with American Presbyterians.

Why did the 'Send Back the Money' campaign fail? Was it just a
passing storm in a teacup? Did it make any contribution to the long
haul towards ridding America of slavery? And did the ethical and
theological issues raised by it have later repercussions in the history
of the Christian church?

The Free Church delegation of 1843 had clearly failed to take
on board the potential explosiveness of gaining credibility in
the slave states of the American South. For many in Scotland by
the early 1840s there was now a feeling that since the campaign
against slavery, in which men such as Andrew Thomson and Ralph

Wardlaw had taken such a leading and well publicised part, had brought the desired result, the issue was closed. Had the delegation not gone to Charleston, almost certainly interest in American slavery would not have been nearly as intense in Scotland. But by the time George Lewis found himself horrified by what he saw of slavery in the raw in Georgia and Alabama, the money from Charleston was already in Free Church hands. His discomfort was increased when he and William Chalmers attended the General Assembly of the Presbyterian Church in Kentucky in May 1844, to learn that there was a ban on the subject of slavery even being raised there.

Having found themselves in that position, the Free Church leadership, as we have seen, attempted to sweep the issue under the carpet. When that became impossible, they pled for an understanding of the difficulties of the American churches, and used the familiar argument for stalling on action by claiming that the situation was too complex to be properly understood by those outside of it. When that didn't work, they relied on fine distinctions of theology and terminology. Slave-holding and slave-having were separated in order that those in the latter category could be absolved of any blame for their situation. Corporate sin, on which they all agreed, was a different matter from individual behaviour, and the varying ways in which slave-owners treated their slaves became the true test for their sinfulness. Thomas Chalmers wanted to separate civic and political institutions from ecclesiastical ones to the extent that he came close to saying that the church should not have the right to comment on the former – a curious position for a church that claimed to have national responsibility, with a heritage from Calvin and Knox, but a position dictated by the corner into which the Free Church had allowed itself to be driven.

Thomas Chalmers held himself aloof from interventions in the Assembly and set out his position solely by correspondence. William Cunningham made no attempt to meet the concerns of the abolitionists whom he regarded with contempt, claiming that they were doing the work of the devil. It was not the last time that he would attribute satanic power to a group of Christians. He later described 'Popery' as 'the masterpiece of Satan – his greatest and most successful scheme for frustrating the designs of the Christian religion'.[2] The Free Church was well aware that the repeal of penal legislation against Roman Catholics in 1829 had widened opportunities for them and presented a perceived threat to Protestants. Catholic emancipation owed much to Daniel O'Connell, the Irish politician who was at that time also the most prominent anti-slavery figure in Britain and Ireland.

William Cunningham may also have had the most to lose if the 'Send Back the Money' campaign had spun out of control. As unofficial leader of the Free Church delegation in 1843, he was in a sense responsible for their journey to America. His host in Princeton, Charles Hodge, held strong views on the danger of losing the support of southern Presbyterians, a position that had been savaged by Douglass in 1846. There was much at stake if a quarrel with the leading lights in the Presbyterian Church had broken out and led to the Americans withdrawing their goodwill towards the Free Church. Thomas Smyth had hinted of this to Chalmers. There was even more at stake if a split had taken place within the Free Church of Scotland. The leadership of the Free Church were agreed on the priority of avoiding that at all costs.

But Robert Candlish was a very different personality. He had a personal commitment to the abolition of slavery that he had proved in the past, and was to do so again. It was said that Abraham Lincoln read a piece by Candlish during the American Civil War and was so moved by it that, he declared that in spite of so much apparent sympathy for the South, Scotland was 'still sound on the question of slavery'. 'Who knows what hand I may have had in freeing the poor negro?' was Candlish's response.[3]

In his Assembly speeches he attempted to meet the concerns and demands of the abolitionists as far as he could. He admitted that both the Free Church and the American churches had failed to take a robust enough position on slavery, and he promised to make as strong representations as possible to the American churches on their duties. He offered, seemingly without consultation with others, to give, for the benefit of the slaves, five times the amount obtained from the South. Of all the leaders of the Free Church he was the only one who admitted that there might be future circumstances when the Church might have to break off fellowship with the American churches. Henry Grey and John Duncan certainly seemed to imply that with great passion at the 1845 Presbytery of Edinburgh, but they were very easily persuaded to accommodate themselves to the Candlish position. And that position was that the unity and peace of the Free Church surmounted everything.

Others who might have been prepared to challenge the official line were sufficiently mollified by Candlish's diplomatic approach. Michael Willis was not a commissioner at the 1846 Assembly and Robert Burns had already left for a teaching post in Toronto. Either could have prevented the total isolation of James Macbeth. And so it was that the only consistent fly in the Free Church ointment at its highest level was to be the minister of Lauriston Free Church in Glasgow. The leadership of the Free Church had managed to blunt opposition by careful tactics, and by emphasis that the abolitionists were not only composed of those in other churches who had a vendetta against the Free Church, but had a fair number of those without religion.

In *The Scots Abolitionists*, Duncan Rice contended that slavery was a convenient issue for the Church of Scotland on the one side, and the churches who had broken links with the State on the other, to use against the Free Church. *The Witness* was to do a fair amount of thundering against 'arrows shot, not against American slaveholders, but against the Free Church'.[4] While it is true that the major figures in the abolitionist movement were ministers of other churches and that only two office bearers of the Free Church Anti-Slavery Society were Free Church ministers, there were in fact hardly any Church of Scotland ministers involved. The church which had been denuded of ministers and congregations by the Disruption, and might have felt it convenient to attack the Free Church on slavery, kept a dignified silence on the matter. Gossip there may have been, and in communities up and down the land there would have been gleeful comments that were reflected in some of the songs. Nevertheless no public advantage was taken by the Church of Scotland from the dilemma faced by the Free Church.

Those who did not keep silent were in the most part from other denominations. Yet men such as George Gilfillan of Dundee, John Ritchie of Edinburgh or Ralph Wardlaw of Glasgow, and women such as Eliza Wigham and her mother-in-law Jane, had a proud record of anti-slavery activity long before the Free Church became involved in the issue. They would have been prepared to attack any church or religious group, including their own, if they found themselves at odds with it on this vital issue of human rights. It is short changing those to the fore in the abolition movement, to suggest that their major concern was to gloat over the Free Church's discomfiture.

On tactics and ideology however, the abolitionists were far more divided, despite Douglass's attempt to span the various groups. Not only was it impossible to create a national anti-slavery campaign, but the substantial public meetings, the slogans on walls and the song sheets in the streets, were like fireworks which produced dramatic sound and light and then just as quickly faded. Both Frederick Douglass and George Thomson knew how to play to the crowds. They found the varied and extreme excursions of Henry. C. Wright a hindrance and an embarrassment, but in the end of the day these were a sideshow. Having said that, the Glasgow Emancipation Society and the Smeal family invested much time and energy in lionising Wright, who became for them almost a greater hero than Douglass.

Frederick Douglass may have had the impression that 'old Scotia boiled like a pot' over the Free Church money, but if it did for a while, the pot soon went off the boil. All that the Free Church had to do was to sit tight and let the furore die down.

The robust fury of the pamphlets that emerged from the Free Church Anti-Slavery Society could not ignite the popular flames of 1846, which were dying embers eighteen months later. With Robert Burns, Michael Willis and James Macbeth all in Canada by the end of the decade, the Free Church establishment were home and dry.

The ethical issues – twentieth-century parallels

The break with fellow Christians who shared the same theological approach was a very serious matter, as the Evangelical Alliance realised. Robert Candlish in the Assembly and Thomas Chalmers in his letter to *The Witness*, recognised the possibility of this, but only if slavery could be judged in such a way that its acceptance by the church entailed a fundamental assault on the very basis of the faith. Clearly James Macbeth and Michael Willis saw it this way, as did John Duncan, until persuaded otherwise. William Cunningham was very clear that it was not so. 'You cannot', he told the 1847 General Assembly, 'convict them (the American Churches) of heresy in respect of slavery; you can only say there is much that is erroneous and defective in their impressions and mode of action'.[5]

This went to the theological heart of the matter and when accepted by the Free Church, it ended any possibility of a break. In 1934 the Confessing Church in Germany declared as 'heretical' the Reichskirk – the official German Church – sanctioned by, and many would say controlled by, the Nazi State. Although it was the anti-Semitic Aryan Decrees that substantially led to this break, there was a parallel with the Free Church in that the Confessing Church regarded any attempt of the state to determine the life and doctrine of the church a *status confessionis* which could not be tolerated.[6]

It was much later that the Confessing Church actively challenged the political and social policies of the Nazi Government – its most famous leader Dietrich Bonhoeffer was executed for supporting the 1944 plot to kill Hitler. Nonetheless, it was the action of the German theologians in the 1930s that provided the impetus for the declaration of the World Alliance of Reformed Churches in 1982 that *apartheid* in South Africa was a heresy. The Assembly of the Alliance meeting in Ottawa, took the position that for Reformed Christians this was a *status confessionis*, and that the two main white Dutch Reformed

Churches in South Africa should be suspended from membership until certain conditions were met.

The conditions were that black Christians should no longer be excluded from church services, especially from Holy Communion, that concrete support in word and deed must be given to those who suffered under *apartheid* and finally that unequivocal Synod resolutions were passed specifically rejecting *apartheid* and committing the church to dismantling the system in both church and politics.

At first sight there would seem to be some parallels with what the Free Church of Scotland was seeking in its remonstrances with the American church. The American churches were urged to support the ordinances of religion for slaves, to take measures to mitigate their suffering, and to work towards eventual emancipation. But the World Alliance of Reformed Churches was calling, as Andrew Thomson had done in 1830, for what today would been termed 'zero tolerance' and for urgent and immediate action to dismantle the whole system.

When the World Alliance defined a *status confessionis* as 'an issue on which it is not possible to differ without seriously jeopardising the integrity of our common confession as Reformed Churches', their position was fundamentally different from that of the Free Church leadership, as Dr Cunningham's rejection of the term 'heresy' indicated.[7] The documentation surrounding the Ottawa Assembly in 1982 along with essays by a number of South African theologians, black and white, was published under the title *Apartheid is a Heresy*.[8] Dr Alan Boesak, the black South African church leader who was elected President of the World Alliance in 1982, was asked in Edinburgh why he had taken so much trouble with the concept of heresy, when *apartheid*, as a crime against humanity, deserved the active striving together of all of goodwill to destroy it.

He replied that the Anti-Apartheid Movement certainly united people of different faiths and none, and added 'but for us in the church because *apartheid* was conceived theologically, it has also to be destroyed theologically'.[9] Although slavery was, with a few glaring exceptions, never theologically justified in Britain, the situation in America was very different. Frederick Douglass and Henry C. Wright in their public meetings instanced many prominent churchmen, not all in the Southern states, who attempted to justify slavery on biblical and theological grounds. For this reason the refusal of leading Free Churchmen, whilst condemning slavery as a general sinful institution, but resisting the ultimate sanctions on those who continued to accept it, arguably found themselves on the wrong side of the moral line. James Macbeth, whether or not his personal sexual morality could be called into question, stood on the other side.

In the Ottawa debate over *apartheid*, the Afrikaans Churches in South Africa, not surprisingly, put up strong resistance. Rev. J.E. Potgieter, Moderator of the Nederduitse Gereformeerde Kerk said that he envied delegates who didn't have to live in a difficult multiracial situation, and asked them to act in the spirit of the constitution and 'deepen and widen fellowship among member churches', rather than suspend them. Professor Johan Heyns, who was to prove a moderate in the style of Thomas Smyth, and was later murdered by extremists, pointed to what he called 'hopeful signs amongst South African churches with regard to *apartheid*, and begged the Alliance not to embark on the dangerous road of 'amputation'. Two delegates from Ireland argued that the course suggested would prevent the repentance called for, and postpone the day when the evil system could be ended. They echoed Dr. Cunningham's contention, and that of *The Witness*, that such radical action in fact damaged the cause of the oppressed and postponed the prospects of emancipation.

Rev. Robert Waters, representing the Congregational Union and the United Free Church of Scotland, stated that these two churches were unanimous in their condemnation of *apartheid*, but questioned whether a brother who behaved badly should be rejected. He and a delegate from Australia pled for a more constructive approach.

This conciliatory move led to a strong reaction from members of the World Alliance, who were barely represented in the Evangelical Alliance and not at all in the Free Church Assembly – the victims of the system. An African minister, Dr Welile Mazamisa, regretted that the focus had been on the two white South African churches, and not on the millions of blacks who were victims of *apartheid*. He challenged the credibility of the World Alliance if the action proposed was not agreed. His uncompromising position echoed that of Frederick Douglass. The difference was that Douglass was never a delegate to an assembly which had responsibility for such a decision.

The proposal to suspend the two white South African churches was adopted by 220 votes to 20 with 12 abstentions. Six delegates from Switzerland, the Netherlands and the United States supported the resolutions without reservation but declined to take a theological position on the use of the words *status confessionis* or heresy.[10]

There were two overall themes which informed the debate in the Free Church and the Evangelical Alliance over churches that accepted slavery in the 1840s, and that in the World Alliance over churches that accepted *apartheid* in the 1980s. One was the theological consideration as to whether the issue was fundamental to the cause, not just of the church, but of the Christian faith. If so, then there was no alternative but to part company, even on a temporary basis, with other Christians. The second was whether the outcome of the issue, which all were united in hope, could be best advanced by the radical act, or threat of it, of breaking fellowship. The Free Church decided on the first that it was not, and on the second that the cause would be damaged by this course. The Evangelical Alliance hovered between the two courses, especially on the second part. The World Alliance of Reformed Churches by a large majority took the view that for theologically and practical reasons a break had to be made.

Of course it was not possible to separate the theological and the practical, for both informed each other. As Frederick Douglass and Dr Mazamisa were at pains to point out, the perspective was very different if you were in the security of a Scottish home or among the conditions on a slave plantation or a black ghetto in South Africa. A similar feeling was echoed in the segregated Southern states a century after slavery, when Dr Martin Luther King was incarcerated in a jail in Birmingham, Alabama. Well meaning white ministers wrote to him asking him to wait until the time was right, as it surely would be, for desegregation. This was an echo of Thomas Smyth's looking for the ending of slavery 'in God's good time', and it seemed to have a persuasive logic.

Dr King's response in his *Letter from Birmingham Jail* drew on the urgency for justice of the Old Testament prophets, when he assured his fellow ministers that waiting meant 'never'. Postponement in grasping the nettle, for him, gave those in whose interests it was to maintain the system, an unlimited breathing space. And subsequent events, until the passing of the Civil Rights Bill and the enforcement of voting rights in the United States, would seem to have proved him right.

Scottish public awareness and the next rounds

In 1846 a writer to *The Witness*, 'Spectator', made an assessment of the Scottish public's attitude to the 'Send Back the Money' campaign:

'Send back the Money' has now become the hue and cry of the day. *The Guardian* may try to throw ridicule and contempt upon the itinerating orators and *The Witness* may disdain to ignore them. But the public mind will be roused and the public indignation will cry out – against the gross inconsistency of men calling themselves Free, patronising and encouraging slavery, of men repudiating all communion with the established ministers of the Church of Scotland on the grounds that they are slaves to the state, and yet hug to their bosoms the clergy and congregations of the churches in America who traffic in human flesh, who prohibit their slaves from reading the scriptures, and pervert the gospel itself to uphold and justify this abominable system.[11]

It was powerful rhetoric, but it was to dissipate all too quickly in the years that followed. The fact that the 'Send Back the Money' campaign, and the controversy within and outside the Assemblies of the Free Church of Scotland, finds little mention in that church's historical accounts, might lead to the conclusion that the whole event was an insignificant storm in a tea-cup. But there are two reasons for modifying that analysis. One is that inconvenient facts that challenge national or group mythology are often left out in the writing of history. It is only in the last few years that the issue of slavery has been touched upon by Scottish historians writing about Scottish history. Despite the fact that Glasgow's eighteenth century wealth was to a large extent built on sugar, tobacco and cotton, and that in 1770 the historian Edward Long reckoned that one-third of the white population of Jamaica, the largest slave island in the West Indies, were Scots, the convenient myth prevailed that 'this horrible traffik', as the slave trade was termed, was a burden of guilt to be laid on English ports such as Liverpool and Bristol.

Secondly, although it is the dramatic events from which we learn history, the tireless action of ordinary people can equally produce a corrosive effect on the great inhumanities. When Nelson Mandela spoke to the crowds in Glasgow city centre in 1992, he admitted that the collapse of the South African economy, the armed struggle, international isolation and the resistance by a new generation of young people, had all been factors in destroying *apartheid*. But he also paid fullsome tribute to the campaigning of ordinary people in Scotland, raising the issues, refusing to believe the propaganda and refusing to buy South African produce. For him, these gave hope to the oppressed, and put cumulative pressure on the *apartheid* Government. The combined efforts of the abolitionists in the 1840s to raise awareness of slavery, may not have produced the results they hoped for, but any tyrannical system is inevitably weakened by its exposure, to say nothing of the hope this gives to many of its victims.

In September 1850 a bill passed through the United States Congress known as the Fugitive Slave Act. It was conceived as a sop to the South, which felt that abolitionists were stealing their property, and was yet another fruitless attempt to avoid the inevitable split in the nation. The sheltering of slaves fleeing to the North was made a Federal offence, and draconian penalties were imposed on any who failed to assist the authorities in their duty of apprehending them and returning them to their masters in the South. There was of course no extradition of self liberated slaves who reached Canada. They were under the protection of Britain, who had abolished slavery in the Empire sixteen years previously.

Abolitionists on the east coast of America realised that their efforts to shelter and conceal slaves would eventually fail, although many paid dearly for their attempts by imprisonment or violence. Instead a number of self liberated African Americans were sent to Britain, where their safety could be guaranteed. Many of them appeared on platforms and large public meetings, held by the revived Scottish abolition societies, once more galvanised into protest. The Scottish public were confronted with some stirring and dramatic escape stories – William 'Box' Brown, who had himself mailed in a container to Philadelphia, and William and his light skinned wife Ellen Craft, who both escaped from Georgia posing as a young white gentleman and his servant.

There was considerable anger at what was seen as an iniquitous law, and many who organised and attended the protest meetings had earlier heard Frederick Douglass describe for them the reality of slavery. Amongst the protesters, and shortly to become a committee member of the new Edinburgh Anti-Slavery Association, was Robert Candlish. The Free Church leader no doubt welcomed the freedom to make his anti-slavery credentials clear. Once again the press reported considerable numbers taking the opportunity to hear these first hand reports from self liberated slaves, to marvel at the courage of the escapees, and deplore their treatment. There was precious little press comment in favour of the American law, and although the anti-slavery groups were now even more divided on either side of the Garrisonian position, the churchmen and women were united in their call for immediate emancipation.

Scots were divided in their sympathies, when Civil War broke out in America in 1861. With so many emigrants from Scotland in the South feeding information home, allied with traditional Scottish support for the underdog, which the South was often seen to be, the issue of slavery was somewhat superseded. Other Scots took commercial advantage, for much of the considerable trade with the South, not least in gun running, had its origins in Glasgow.[12] But none of this eclipsed the basic sympathy for the oppressed that is deep in the Scottish psyche, and which informed its religious life from the earliest of the petitions in 1788 against the slave trade to the churches part in the campaign against *apartheid* two centuries further on. The 'Send Back the Money' campaign may appear to have been no more than a passing and failed storm. The fact that Anti-Slavery International records the sobering statistic that there are more slaves in the world today than ever before may seem to reinforce this. Yet it was a significant building block in public awareness, and in solidarity with those far away, in a struggle that needs to be renewed in each generation.

Notes

Introduction: A Church with Freedom but no Money

1. In Presbyterian church government the Moderator is elected for a year to represent the Church, but above all to preside over the annual General Assembly, the highest authority in the Church.
2. Thomas Brown, *Annals of the Disruption* (Edinburgh: Macniven and Wallace, 1893) pp. 90–91.
3. J.H.S. Burleigh, *A Church History of Scotland* (Oxford: University Press, 1960) , p. 339.
4. *Annals of the Disruption* p. 20n.
5. Ibid; p. 351.
6. *Annals of the Disruption,* Appendix III. p. 816.

Chapter 1: A Delegation Warmly Received

1. An account of this is to be found in Donald Macleod's *Gloomy Memories of the Highlands of Scotland versus Mrs Harriet Beecher Stowe's Sunny Memories or a Faithful Picture of the Extirpation of the Celtic Race from the Highlands of Scotland* (Edinburgh: 1841)
2. Old Testament or Hebrew Bible: Isaiah Chapter 5.v.8 Authorised Version.
3. Cited in Ian Henderson, *Scotland: Kirk and People* (Edinburgh: Lutterworth, 1969) p. 70.
4. Robert Rainey and James Mackenzie, *The Life of William Cunningham* (London: T. Nelson, 1871) p. 206.
5. The comments on Cunningham, Burns, Lewis and Ferguson are from the diaries of Professor Alexander between 30 Dec 1843 and 9 Apr 1844. *40 Years Familiar* Letters of Rev. J.W.Alexander D.D. ed. Rev John Hall (New York: Charles Scribner's 1860) pp. 386-392.
6. The account of Burns's and (later) Lewis's interview (with President John Tyler are from *Impressions of America and the American Churches from the Journal of Rev. G. Lewis, one of the Deputation of the Free Church of Scotland to the United States* (Edinburgh: W.P. Kennedy, 1845) pp. 78–79, 108, 127, 129, 146, 159, 295, 297.
7. George Lewis's assessment of American slavery is found in the later part of his book and the quotes are from pp. 412, 415 and 417.
8. *Letter from the Executive Committee of the American and Foreign Anti-Slavery Society to the Commissioners of the Free Church of Scotland* (Edinburgh: Myles Macphail, 1844)
9. Patrick Hamilton was the first Protestant martyr in Scotland in 1527. George Wishart suffered a similar fate in 1546. Alexander Henderson

died in his bed after a colourful career which saw him take a leading part in the 1638 *National Covenant* against King Charles the First's attempt to impose Bishops on the Kirk. Andrew Thomson, Minister of St. George's Church in Edinburgh, but for his sudden death in 1831 would undoubtedly have been the leader of the Free Church.
10. *40 Years Familiar*, p. 392.

Chapter 2: The Elephant in the Room

1. *Proceedings of the General Assembly of the Free Church of Scotland held in Edinburgh May 1844* (Edinburgh: William Whyte, 1844) pp. 64–68.
2. Ibid; pp. 69–70.
3. Ibid; pp. 71–76.
4. Ibid; pp. 76–77.
5. Minutes of the Glasgow Emancipation Society. Smeal Collection, Mitchell Library, Glasgow Reel 1. p. 238.
6. Ibid.
7. Ibid; p. 245.
8. Ibid; 21 May 1844 p. 257.
9. *Proceedings of the Free Church General Assembly* p. 163. An 'Overture' in Presbyterian Church government is similar to a 'Petition' which is normally from an individual.
10. Ibid; pp.163–164.
11. Princeton Students to Edinburgh Missionary Association, 30 Sep 1843. New College Library, Edinburgh Special Collections AA.33.32.3.
12. The Committee's Report to the September 1844 Commission of Assembly is printed in the Preliminary Section of the *Report of the Proceedings of the General Assembly* in 1846, pp. 4,5.

Chapter 3: Chalmers and Smyth – Tensions across the Atlantic

1. Thomas Smyth to Thomas Chalmers, 24 May 1844. New College Library, Edinburgh Chalmers Papers CHA4.315.64.
2. J. W. Blessinghame ed. *The Frederick Douglas Papers – Speeches, Debates and Interviews* (New Haven: Yale University Press, 1979) Vol 1. p. 297n. Candlish joined numerous clergy in Scotland and England in this protest which reached the newspapers in Charleston. He was later to support the action of the more famous John Brown at Harper's Ferry in 1859.
3. Michael Willis was a maverick but well respected figure in the Free Church. Originally ordained as minister of Albion Street Secession Church, he joined the Church of Scotland in 1839, then the Free Church, being particularly active in supporting the breakaway Presbyterian Church of Canada.
4. Ed Macey and Frederick Porcher, *Haunted Charleston* (Charleston : The History Press, 2004) p. 78.
5. Erskine Clarke, *Thomas Smyth, Moderate of the Old South'*. ThD. Dissertation, Union Seminary 1970. American National Biography (Oxford: University Press, 1998) pp. 331–332.
6. The Acts of the British Parliament Abolishing the Slave Trade and

Slavery itself were passed in 1807 and 1833.

7. Thomas Chalmers, *A Few Thoughts on the Abolition of Colonial Slavery* (Collins: Glasgow 1826).
8. I am indebted for information about family connections with the slave trade to Professor S.J. Brown author of *Thomas Chalmers and the Godly Commonwealth in Scotland* (Oxford: University Press, 1983).
9. Andrew Thomson, made a key speech in October 1831 calling for immediate abolition of slavery in the British Empire. It had a great impact in moving the abolition campaign to new urgency in Britain and Thomson was extensively quoted in abolitionist circles in the United States and pejoratively amongst the planters in the West Indies. He died suddenly in 1831.
10. Elihu Burritt to Thomas Chalmers 20 Dec 1843, Chalmers Papers CHA. 306.74.
11. George Lewis to Thomas Chalmers 1 Jun 1844, Chalmers Papers CHA4. 314.26.
12. Thomas Smyth to Thomas Chalmers 29 Aug 1844, Chalmers Papers CHA. 4.315.66.
13. George Shepperson, 'Notes and Documents. Thomas Chalmers, the Free Church of Scotland and the South', *Journal of Southern History* 1951 pp. 517–537.
14. Rev. William Hanna, *Memoirs of the Life and Writings of Dr.Thomas Chalmers* (Constable Edinburgh 1862) p. 581.
15. Edinburgh Emancipation Society to Thomas Chalmers 4 Dec 1844 NC Chalmers Papers CHA4.312.77.
16. A.H. Abel and F.J. Klingberg eds. *A Side Light on Anglo-American Relations 1839–1858* (Washington 1927) p. 196 cited by George Shepperson, *Notes and Documents*, p. 520.
17. *The Witness*, May 1844.
18. Thomas Smyth, *The Character of the Late Thomas Chalmers and the Lessons of his Life from Personal Recollections* (Charleston, 1847).

Chapter 4: Keeping a Lid on the Volcano

1. Glasgow Emancipation Society Minutes, 1 July 1844. p. 259.
2. Ibid, 1 Aug 1844 p. 260.
3. *Annual Reports of the Glasgow Emancipation Society* Smeal Collection Mitchell Library. Reel.2 p. 16. The churches mentioned were the Reformed Presbyterian Church, The Associate Synod, the General Associate Church and the Associate Reformed Church. None of these, as Dr Burns admitted, were numerically anywhere near the mainstream Presbyterian Church. John Ritchie, known as 'radical John', was a fiercely independent minister who had since the beginning of the century been zealous for the abolition of slavery. After the death of Andrew Thomson in 1831, he had assumed a key role in the Scottish movement, more actively involved in *The Glasgow Emancipation Society* than among the Edinburgh abolitionists.
4. Glasgow Emancipation Society Minutes 18 Nov 1844 pp. 267–269.
5. 'Sawder', or more usually spelt 'Souder' was a Scots word for alleviating

pain or settling a quarrel.

6. *The Life of Dr. Cunningham* pp. 24–30.
7. *Minutes of the Free Church of Scotland, Presbytery of Edinburgh* 14 Mar 1845 West Register House, Edinburgh CH/111/25 p. 275; Reports in *Edinburgh Advertiser, Caledonian Mercury*.
8. Glasgow Emancipation Society Minutes 17 Mar 1845 p. 270; Henry C. Wright, *American Slavery proved to be Theft and Robbery which no circumstances can justify or palliate. With remarks on the speeches of Rev. Doctors Cunningham and Candlish before the Free Presbytery of Edinburgh.* (Edinburgh: Quinten Dalrymple (1845) pp. 5, 7, 9, 11, 23.
9. *The Witness*, 22 Mar 1845.
10. *Proceedings of the General Assembly of the Free Church of Scotland held at Edinburgh May 1845* (Edinburgh: W.P. Kennedy, 1845) 2 Jun 1845 pp. 256–258.
11. The text of the American response is to be found in the *Report of the Proceedings of the General Assembly on Saturday, May 30 and Monday June 1, 1846, regarding the Relations of the Free Church of Scotland and the Presbyterian Churches of America* (Edinburgh: John Johnstone, 1846) pp. 8–11.

Chapter 5: 'Douglass has blawn sic a flame'

1. Douglass to Jackson 29 Jan 1846. Boston Public Library A.1.2 v.16.
2. Cited in George Shepperson, 'Frederick Douglass and Scotland', *Journal of Negro History*, 1953. p. 307.
3. *Frederick Douglass Papers* Vol.1. 15 Jan 1846, Glasgow p. 138.
4. Ibid; 30 Jan 1846 Dundee, pp.144-156; *Report of the Speeches delivered at a Soirée in Honour of Messrs Douglass, Buffen and Wright* (Dundee, 1846) pp. 21–29.
5. *Frederick Douglass Papers* Vol 1. 12 Feb 1846 Arbroath , pp. 156–164.
6. Ibid; 24 Mar 1846, Ayr, pp. 195-204; 17 Apr 1846, Paisley, pp. 215–231; 25 Apr, Paisley, pp. 240–243.
7. Rev. John Macnaughton, Minister of the Free Church of Paisley, was a staunch defender of the Free Church's position, expressed in a pamphlet which he published *The Free Church and American Slavery: Slanders against the Free Church met and answered.* (Paisley, 1846)
8. *Frederick Douglass Papers* Vol 1. 25 Apr 1846, Paisley, pp. 241–242.
9. Ibid; 23 Sep1846, Paisley, pp. 426–433.
10. *The Scottish Guardian* 11 Apr 1846.
11. Matthew 23.23. Jesus accuses the Pharisees of paying their tithes of these crops and neglecting the qualities of justice and mercy.
12. *American Slavery:Report of a Meeting held at Finsbury Chapel, Moorfields, to receive Frederick Douglass, The American Slave on Friday 22 May 1846,* (London 1846) p. 27. Rev. John Campbell was a Scottish born and educated Congregational minister in London.
13. Frederick Douglass, *My Bondage and my Freedom* (New York: Miller, Orton and Co. 1855) p. 381.
14. Eliza Wigham, *The Anti-Slavery Cause in America and its Martyrs* (London: A. W. Bennett, 1863) Preface.

15. Douglas to Jackson 29 Jan 1846; Douglas to Webb 10 Feb 1846. Boston Public Library A.1.2 v16.
16. *Anti-Slavery Songs*, Bodleian Library, Oxford, G.Pamph 2586(3).

Chapter 6: War, Drink, the Sabbath, and the 1846 Assembly

1. H.C. Wright, *American Slavery proved to be Theft and Robbery; The Dissolution of the American Union Demanded by Justice and Humanity as the Incurable Enemy of Liberty* (London: Chapman Brothers, 1846).
2. H.C. Wright, *First Day Sabbath not of Divine Appointment with the opinions of Calvin, Luther, Belsham, Melanchthon, Barclay, Paley and others* (Glasgow: William Brown, 1846).
3. D. Tomkins, *The Yankee Looking Glass* (Edinburgh: 1846); A Close Observer, *Letter to the Managers of Rose Street Secession Church and College Street Relief Church Denouncing their Conduct for Admitting Infidels and Sabbath-Breakers to Slander the Free Church* (Edinburgh:1846).
4. H.C. Wright, *Send Back that Money – To the Members and Ministers of the Free Church of Scotland* (1846) Many of the short pamphlets written by Henry C. Wright are to be found in the National Library of Scotland 1.89.2.
5. *The Dissolution of the American Union* , p. 43.
6. *Send Back the Money*, reprinted from the *Fifeshire Journal* of 7 May and 14 May (Cupar, 1846).
7. A printed copy of the letter is in the National Library of Scotland 1.82.4.
8. *Agitation Against the Free Church Acknowledged Slander by H.C. Wright against the Free Church Ministers, Elders, and Congregation at Hawick* (Glasgow: J.R .Macnair, 1846).
9. *Report of the Proceedings of the General Assembly regarding the Relations of the Free Church and the Presbyterian Churches of America* (Edinburgh: John Johnstone, 1846) p. 13.
10. Voluntarism was a principle adopted by many Secession Churches who distanced themselves from all Established churches, which many regarded as unscriptural and immoral, and denied their Divine authority. Henry C. Wright's own convictions sat comfortably with Voluntarism. The Free Church, and especially Dr Thomas Chalmers, were appalled by this and wanted to ensure that they were committed to Establishment. Chalmers said at the first Free Church Assembly 'Though we quit the establishment . . . a vitiated Establishment, we would rejoice in returning to a pure one'.
11. *Report of the Proceedings of the General Assembly*, p. 28.
12. Ibid; p. 33.
13. Ibid; p. 33–36.
14. Ibid; pp. 36-45.
15. Mary Welsh to Maria Weston Chapman 17 May 1846. Cited in Clare Taylor, *British and American Abolitionists – An Episode in Transatlantic Understanding* (Edinburgh: University Press, 1974) p. 201.
16. *Caledonian Mercury*, 7 May 1846.
17. *A Review of the Proceedings of a minority of the Town Council of the City of*

Edinburgh (Edinburgh: James Johnston, 1846).
18. A.Cameron, *The Free Church and Her Accusers in the Matter of American Slavery; being a letter to Mr George Thompson Regarding His Recent Appearances in this City* (Edinburgh, 1846). Andrew Cameron was employed to undertake literary work on the staff of The *Witness*. Cameron assumed many of the editorial duties at this time. He was ordained in 1866.
19. C.D. Rice, *The Scots Abolitionists* (Baton Rouge: State University of Louisiana Press, 1982) p. 139

Chapter 7: Ballads and Broadsheets

1. In the earlier campaign against the British Slave Trade many petitions from Scotland to Parliament in 1792 warned that the continuation of the 'accursed trade' would risk divine vengeance on the nation.
2. Abolitionists knew that although audiences would be shocked at the severity of punishment inflicted on all slaves there was a particular revulsion against the indecent exposure of female bodies to a flogging, administered very often in plantation homes by the mistress.
3. There was almost more hostility between the Free Church and Dissenters than with the Church of Scotland. Chalmers strongly opposed those whose ecclesiastical allegiance was totally divorced from the state.
4. John Ritchie the veteran abolitionist and minister of the United Secession Church in Potterrow, Edinburgh.
5. Strangely the word 'priest' is often used in the eighteenth and nineteenth centuries for Reformed ministers in Scotland. Robert Burns in *Holy Willies Prayer* employs the term.
6. Although George Thompson's record of transparency over money taken at meetings left something to be desired, there is no evidence that he ever patronised Douglass in this way.
7. Until well into the twentieth century the system of an annual 'pew rent' for a seat in the Kirk was common in the Church of Scotland.
8. This could well be a reference to Rev. Dr Thomas Smyth of Charleston.
9. *American Slavery: Report of a Public Meeting held at Finsbury Chapel, Moorfields, to receive Frederick Douglass the American Slave on Friday 22nd May 1846* (London: 1846) p. 31.
10. *Knight v Wedderburn* in the Court of Session, An excellent account of this is given in the novel by James Robertson, Joseph *Knight* (London, Fourth Estate, 2003).

Chapter 8: The Irish Take a Firmer Stand

1. The major split in abolitionism was between those who supported the position of William Lloyd Garrison that slavery could not be ended by constitutional means and the more conservative position espoused (despite his radical rhetoric) by Frederick Douglass to seek abolition within the American constitution. There was much tension between the two groups in the late 1840s and onwards. Extensive research on 'Thomas Smyth, Frederick Douglass and the Belfast Anti-Slavery

162

'Send Back the Money!'

Campaign' was undertaken by the late Professor J.F. Maclear of the University of Minnesota and published in the *Proceedings of the South Carolina Historical Society* (Charleston,1979) pp. 286–297.

2. *The Frederick Douglass Papers* Vol 1. pp. 34–36, 55, 58, 112,113, Revd Daniel Sharp was a Baptist minister in Boston. He was, like Smyth, an emigrant from Britain and although he made clear his dislike of slavery, he was passionately opposed to the idea of excommunicating slave-owners.
3. *British and American Abolitionists.* pp. 247, 254, 258.
4. Thomas Smyth's life is chronicled in *Autobiographical Notes, Letters and Reflections by Thomas Smyth D.D.;* ed. Louisa Cheves Stoney (Charleston, 1914) I am indebted for information on this period to Emeritus Professor Erskine Clarke of Columbia Seminary, Decatur, Georgia
5. Mary Cunningham to Thomas Smyth, *Autobiographical Notes* pp.364-367.
6. George Thompson on 4 June 1846 proposed the formation of the Scottish Anti-Slavery Society based in Edinburgh in an attempt to unify abolitionists in Scotland. It petered out within two years.
7. James Robertson to Thomas Smyth, 1, 6, 23 Jul; 11 Aug 1846. Thomas Smyth to James Robertson, 2 Jul; 7 Aug 1846, Library of the South Carolina Historical Society, Charleston.
8. *Autobiographical Notes, Letters and Reflections,* p. 367.
9. Cooke was a close friend of Thomas Chalmers and had attempted to broker negotiations with the London government prior to the Disruption. He supported the Free Church but was unhappy about any splits and described himself as a 'minister of the Church of Scotland' as well as Ireland. He withdrew from the Assembly in disagreement with its policy over Parliament. Helpful information about Irish Presbyterians and the slavery issue is to be found in Douglas C. Riach, *Ireland and the Campaign Against American Slavery 1830–1860,* unpublished PhD. Thesis, University of Edinburgh 1975.
10. *Caledonian Mercury* 20 Aug 1846.
11. Cited by Riach, *Ireland and the Campaign* pp. 306–307.

Chapter 9: Evangelicals and Abolitionists – Houses Divided

1. *Evangelical Alliance – Report of the Proceedings of the Conference held at Freemason's Hall, London, from August 19th to September 2nd inclusive. Published by Order of the Conference.*(London: Partridge and Oakley 1847) The pages which deal with the debate on slavery are 286-475
2. *Ibid;* pp. 485–487.
3. *Report of the Proceedings of the Great Anti-Slavery Meeting held in Rev. Mr. William Cairns' Church, on Wednesday 23rd September 1846 including the speeches of Wm. Lloyd Garrison Esq. Taken in shorthand by Cincinnatus* (Paisley, 1846)
4. *Caledonian Mercury* 28 Sep 1846.
5. *Slavery, the Evangelical Alliance, and the Free Church: An Address delivered in Glasgow, Scotland on 30 September 1846.* Text in The *Frederick Douglass Papers Vol.1.* pp. 441–453

6. A detailed treatment of the divisions in the American and British Anti-Slavery Societies is found in *The Scots Abolitionists* pp. 115–151.
7. *Address to the Office-Bearers and Members of the Free Church of Scotland on the Present Connexion with the Slaveholding Churches of America. From the Committee of the Free Church anti-Slavery Society* (Edinburgh: Charles Ziegler,1847); *The Scots Abolitionists,* p.249.
8. Ibid; p. 9.
9. This is an exact quotation from Thomson's speech in the Assembly Rooms in Edinburgh on 19 Oct 1830 calling for immediate emancipation 'whatever the consequences'.

Chapter 10: The Last Battles and Hunting 'the Brave Macbeth'

1. *Proceedings of the General Assembly of the Free Church of Scotland held at Edinburgh May 1847* (Edinburgh: John Grieg & Son, 1847).
2. *Strictures on the Proceedings of The Free Church of Scotland regarding Communion with the Slave-Holding Churches of America, respectfully addressed to the Office-Bearers and Members of That Church from the Committee of the Free Church Anti-Slavery Society* (Edinburgh: Charles Ziegler, 1847).
3. It was probably this speech which caused Thomas Smyth to write such a strong letter to Thomas Chalmers (See Chapter 3).
4. *Strictures on the Proceedings* pp. 17, 18.
5. G. Gilfillan, *The Debasing and Demoralising Influence of Slavery on All and Everything Connected with it: A Lecture*;. G. Jeffrey, *The Pro-Slavery Character of the American Churches*; I. Nelson, *Slavery Supported by the American Churches and Countenanced by Recent Proceedings in the Free Church of Scotland, A Lecture*; D. Young, *Slavery Forbidden by the Word of God, a Lecture.* All four pamphlets were published by Charles Ziegler in Edinburgh, 1847.
6. *Proceedings of the General Assembly of the Free Church of Scotland held at Edinburgh May 1848* (Edinburgh: W.P. Kennedy 1848).
7. *The Debasing and Demoralising Influence of Slavery* p. 13.
8. James Macbeth, *No Fellowship with Slave-holders. A calm review of the Debate on Slavery in the Free Church Assembly of 1846 addressed respectfully to the Assembly of 1847 and to members and Kirk Sessions of the Free Church* (Edinburgh: John Johnston & Charles Ziegler 1846*); The Church and the Slaveholder or Light and Darkness. An attempt to prove from the Word of God and from Reason that to hold property in Man is a flagrant crime and demands Excommunication, earnestly and respectfully addressed to members of the approaching Assembly of the Free Church of Scotland and to the Churches generally* (Edinburgh: John Johnston 1847).
9. *No Fellowship with Slaveholders,* pp 10,11. The term ' Erastian' originates from Thomas Erastus, a sixteenth-century German theologian who held that the church should be under the control of the state. The obvious irony, which Macbeth pointed out, was that having freed themselves from state control, the Free Church excused the American churches for accepting slavery on the grounds that it was state law.
10. Ibid; pp. 19, 20, 23, 25, 27.

11. *The Church and the Slaveholder or Light and Darkness* pp. 4, 9, 29, 32.
12. A 'libel' is a term in Presbyterian church law meaning a 'charge' against someone, for 'immoral conduct or error in doctrine'.
13. Minutes of the Free Presbytery of Glasgow, 20 Mar, 7 Jun, 14, Aug, 1, 8 Nov 1848, 29 Mar 1849... Mitchell Library, Glasgow.CH3. 146.34
14. Minutes of the Free Synod of Glasgow and Ayr 23 May -2 June 1849. National Archives, Edinburgh C3/634/1; *Proceedings of the General Assembly of the Free Church of Scotland held at Edinburgh May 1849 and 1850* (Edinburgh: John Grieg 1849, 1851) Jun 1849, Jun 1850.
15. *A Real Statement of the Secret and Concluding Debate in the Assembly on Mr. Macbeth's case . . . by a Lover of Justice and a Member of the Free Church* (Glasgow: 1849) cited in Rice, *The Scots Abolitionist* p.128n.

Chapter 11:
A Passing Storm in a Teacup or the Shape of Things to Come?

1. Eng. 'Facts are fellows that will not be overturned / and cannot be disputed'. From his poem *A Dream* (1776).
2. *The Life of Dr Cunningham*, p. 313.
3. Jean Watson, *The Life of Dr. Candlish* (Edinburgh: James Gemmell 1882) p. 95.
4. *The Witness* 8 Jul 1846.
5. *Report of the Proceedings of the General Assembly 1846*, p. 44.
6. Literal meaning is 'a state of confessing'. It dated back to the struggle between the Reformers and the Emperor Charles V. in Europe in the mid sixteenth century.
7. The history and theological implications of *Status Confessionis* was interpreted in a paper for the World Alliance by Dutch theologian Dr Karel Blei. K. Blei, 'Apartheid as a Status Confessionis' in *Studies from the World Alliance of Reformed Churches* Vol.25 (1994).
8. *Apartheid is a Heresy*, ed. J. De Gruchy and C. Villa-Vicencio (Guildford: Lutterworth Press, 1983).
9. In conversation with the author.
10. *Proceedings of the 21st General Council of the WARC* www.warc.ch/where/21gc/proced/html.
11. *The Witness* 2 May 1846.
12. An account of the most dramatic example of this is given in Eric.J.Graham, *Clyde Built: Blockade Runners, Cruisers, and Armoured Rams of the American Civil War* (Edinburgh: Birlinn, 2006)

Bibliography

Newspapers, Journals and Collections

Bodleian Library, Oxford
Border Watch
Caledonian Mercury
Chalmers Papers, New College Library, Edinburgh
Douglass Papers, Boston Public Library
Dundee Courier
Edinburgh Advertiser
Evening Packet and Correspondent, Dublin
Glasgow Examiner
Glasgow Herald
Journal of Negro History
Journal of Southern History
National Archives, Edinburgh
Northern Warder
Northern Whig
Princeton Review
Scottish Guardian
Scottish Historical Review
The Liberator (Boston)
The Witness
The Warder

Documents

A Real Statement of the Secret and Concluding Debate in the Assembly on Mr.Macbeth's case... by a Lover of Justice and a Member of the Free Church (Glasgow: 1849)

A Review of the Proceedings of a minority of the Town Council of the City of Edinburgh (Edinburgh: James Johnstone, 1846)

Address to the Office-Bearers and Members of the Free Church of Scotland on the Present Connexion with the Slaveholding Churches of America From the Committee of the Free Church Anti-Slavery Society (Edinburgh:Charles Ziegler, 1847)

Agitation Against the Free Church. Acknowledged Slander by H.C. Wright against the Free Church Ministers, Elders, and Congregation at Hawick (Glasgow: J.R.Macnair, 1846)

American Slavery: Report of a Meeting held at Finsbury Chapel, Moorfields, to receive Frederick Douglass the American Slave on Friday 22nd May 1846 (London, 1846)

Annual Reports of the Glasgow Emancipation Society, Smeal Collection, Mitchell Library, Glasgow. Reel 2.

Anti-Slavery Songs, Bodleian Library, Oxford

Evangelical Alliance – Report of the Proceedings of the Conference held at Freemason's Hall, London, from August 19th to September 2nd inclusive. Published by Order of the Committee (London: Partridge and Oakley, 1847)

Letter from the Executive Committee of the American and Foreign Anti-Slavery Society to the Commissioners of the Free Church of Scotland (Edinburgh: Myles Macphail, 1844)

Letter to Edinburgh Missionary Association from Princeton Students 30 Sep 1843

Minutes of the Free Church of Scotland Presbytery of Edinburgh

Minutes of the Free Church of Scotland Presbytery of Glasgow.

Minutes of the Glasgow Emancipation Society Committee.

Proceedings of the General Assembly of the Free Church of Scotland held in Edinburgh - May 1844 (Edinburgh: William Whyte, 1844)

May 1845 (Edinburgh: W.P. Kennedy, 1845)

May 1847 (Edinburgh: John Grieg & Son, 1847)

May 1848 (Edinburgh: W.P. Kennedy, 1848)

May 1849 (Edinburgh: John Grieg, 1849)

May 1850 (Edinburgh: John Grieg, 1851)

Proceedings of the 21st General Council of the World Alliance of Reformed Churches www. Warc.ch/where/21gc/proced/html

Report of the Proceedings of the General Assembly regarding the Relations of the Free Church and the Presbyterian Churches of America (Edinburgh: John Johnstone, 1846).

Report of the Proceedings of the Great Anti-Slavery Meeting held in Rev.Mr.William Cairns' Church on Wednesday 23rd September 1846 including the Speeches of Wm. Lloyd Garrison Esq. Taken in Shorthand by Cincinnatus (Paisley, 1846)

Report of the Speeches delivered at a Soiree in Honour of Messrs Douglass, Buffen, and Wright (Dundee, 1846)

Send Back the Money reprinted from *Fifeshire Journal* (Cupar, 1846)

Strictures on the Proceedings of The Free Church of Scotland regarding Communion with the Slave-Holding Churches of America, respectfully addressed to the Office-Bearers and Members of That Church from the Committee of the Free Church Anti-Slavery Society (Edinburgh: Charles Ziegler, 1847)

Books and Pamphlets before 1865

Cameron, A., *The Free Church and Her Accusers in the Matter of American Slavery; being a letter to Mr.George Thompson Regarding His Recent Appearances in this City* (Edinburgh, 1846)

Chalmers, T., *A Few Thoughts on the Abolition of Colonial Slavery* (Glasgow: Collins, 1826)

Close Observer, *Letter to the Managers of Rose Street Secession Church and College Street Relief Church Denouncing their Conduct for Admitting Infidels and Sabbath-Breakers to Slander the Free Church* (Edinburgh, 1846)

Douglass, F., *My Bondage and My Freedom* (New York: Miller, Ortan and Co, 1855)

Gilfillan, G., *The Debasing and Demoralising Influence of Slavery on All and Everything Connected with it: A Lecture* (Edinburgh: Charles Ziegler, 1847)

Hall, J., ed. *40 Years Familiar – Letters of Rev. J.W. Alexander* (New York: Charles Scribner's, 1860)

Hanna, J., *Memoirs of the Life and Writings of Dr.Thomas Chalmers* (Edinburgh: Constable, 1862)

Jeffrey, G. *The Pro-Slavery Character of the American Churches* (Edinburgh: Charles Ziegler, 1847)

Macleod, D., *Gloomy Memories of the Highlands of Scotland versus Mrs. Harriet Beecher Stowe's Sunny Memories* (Edinburgh, 1841)

Nelson, I., *Slavery Supported by the American Churches and Countenanced by Recent Proceedings in the Free Church of Scotland, A Lecture* (Edinburgh: Charles Ziegler, 1847)

Lewis, G., *Impressions of America and the American Churches from the Journal of Rev.G.Lewis, one of the Deputation of the Free Church of Scotland to the United States* (Edinburgh: W.P.Kennedy, 1845)

Macbeth, J., *No Fellowship with Slave-holders. A calm review of the Debate on Slavery in the Free Church Assembly of 1846 addressed respectfully to the Assembly of 1847 and to members and Kirk Sessions of the Free Church* (Edinburgh: John Johnston & Charles Ziegler 1846)
The Church and the Slaveholder or Light and Darkness. An attempt to prove from the Word of God and from Reason that to hold property in Man is a flagrant crime and demands Excommunication, earnestly and respectfully addressed to members of the approaching Assembly of the Free Church of Scotland and to the Churches generally (Edinburgh: John Johnstone 1847).

Macnaughton, J., *The Free Church and American Slavery: Slanders against the Free Church met and answered* (Paisley: 1846)

Smyth, T., *Character of the late Thomas Chalmers and the Lessons of his Life from Personal Recollections* (Charleston, 1847)

Tomkins, D., *The Yankee Looking Glass* (Edinburgh, 1846)

Wigham, E., *The Anti-Slavery Cause in America and Its Martyrs* (London: A.W. Bennett, 1863)

Wright, H.C., *American Slavery Proved to be Theft and Robbery which no circumstance can justify or palliate* (Edinburgh: Quinten Dalrymple, 1845)
First Day Sabbath not of Divine Appointment, with the opinions of Calvin, Luther, Belsham, Melancthon, Paley and others (Glasgow: William Brown, 1846)
Send Back That Money – to Members and Ministers of the Free Church of Scotland (1846) National Library of Scotland.
The Dissolution of the American Union Demanded by Justice and Humanity as the Incurable Enemy of Liberty (London: Chapman Brothers, 1846)

Young, D., *Slavery Forbidden by the Word of God, a Lecture* (Edinburgh: Charles Ziegler, 1847).

Books, Articles and Pamphlets after 1865

Abel A.H. and Klingsberg F.Ceds. *A Side Light on Anglo American Relations 1939-1858* (Washington DC: 1927)

American National Biography (Oxford: University Press, 1998)

Blei, K., 'Apartheid as a Status Confessionis,' *Studies from the World Alliance of Reformed Churches Vol.25* (1994)

Blessinghame J.W., ed. *The Frederick Douglas Papers – Speeches, Debates and Interviews* (New Haven: Yale University Press, 1979)

Blackett, R.J.M., *Building an Anti-Slavery Wall: Black Americans in the Atlantic Abolitionist Movement Baton Rouge*, (Louisiana State University, 1983)

Brown, S.J., *Thomas Chalmers and the Godly Commonwealth in Scotland* (Oxford: University Press, 1983)

Brown, T., *Annals of the Disruption* (Edinburgh: Macniven and Wallace, 1893)

Burleigh, J.S., *A Church History of Scotland* (Oxford: University Press, 1960)

Clarke, E., *Thomas Smyth, Moderate of the Old South.'* Unpublished. ThD. Dissertation, Union Seminary, Virginia 1970.

Clarke, E., *Our Southern Zion* (Tuscaloosa: University of Alabama Press, 1996)

De Gruchy, J. and Villa-Vicencio ed. *Apartheid is a Heresy* (Guildford: Lutterworth Press, 1983)

Graham, E.J., *Clyde Built: Blockade Runners, Cruisers, and Armoured Rams of the American Civil War* (Edinburgh: Birlinn, 2006)

Henderson, I., *Scotland Kirk and People* (Edinburgh: Lutterworth Press, 1969)

Macey, E., and Porcher, F., *Haunted Charleston* (Charleston: The History Press, 2004)

Maclear, J.F., 'Thomas Smyth, Frederick Douglass, and the Belfast Anti-Slavery Campaign' in *The Proceedings of the South Carolina Historical Society* (Charleston, 1979)

Rainey, R., & .Mackenzie, J., *The Life of William Cunningham* (London: T. Nelson, 1871)

Rice, C.D., *The Scots Abolitionists* (Baton Rouge, State University of Louisiana Press, 1982)

Riach, D., *Ireland and the Campaign Against American Slavery 1830-1860.* Unpublished PhD Thesis. University of Edinburgh, 1985.

Robertson, J., *Joseph Knight* (London:Fourth Estate, 2003)

Stoney, L.C., ed. *Autobiographical Notes, Letters and Reflections by Thomas Smyth D.D.* (Charleston, 1914)

Taylor, C., *British and American Abolitionists. An Episode in Transatlantic Understanding* (Edinburgh: University Press, 1974)

Shepperson, G., 'Notes and Documents. Thomas Chalmers, the Free Church of Scotland and the South' in *Journal of Southern History*, Vol 27 Nov 1951. 'The Free Church and American Slavery' in *Scottish Historical Review*, Vol. 30. Oct 1951.
'Frederick Douglass and Scotland' in *Journal of Negro History*, Vol. 38. July 1953.

Watson, J. *Life of Dr.Candlish* (Edinburgh: James Gemmell, 1882)

Index